Keeping Quail

Katie Thear

Keeping Quail

First edition: 1987
Second edition: 1994
Third edition: 1998
Fourth edition: 2005, 2007

Copyright © 1987, 1994, 1998, 2005, 2007 Katie Thear

Published by Broad Leys Publishing Ltd

A catalogue record for this book is available from the British Library.

ISBN: 978 0906137 38 3

Outside front cover: Fawn Japanese Coturnix hen.

Outside back cover: Top - Tuxedo, Bobwhite and White Coturnix.
Middle - Eggs of Coturnix layers.
Bottom - Chinese Painted male

Unless otherwise stated, the photographs were taken by the author.

For details of other publications please see page 96.

Broad Leys Publishing Ltd
1 Tenterfields,
Newport, Saffron Walden,
Essex CB11 3UW, UK.
Tel/Fax: 01799 541065
E-mail: kdthear@btinternet.com
Website: www.blpbooks.co.uk

Contents

Introduction

"Are they birds of prey?"
"No, they're partridges."
(Two ladies looking at Coturnix quails at Ardingly Show. 1986)

The first edition of this book was published in 1987, with subsequent publications in 1994 and 1998. It has sold all over the world and, as a result, I have received letters from many different countries. I am grateful to all those who have sent in suggestions and contributions, not only for previous editions but also for this new fourth edition.

Quail are classified as game birds, sharing the same family as pheasants and partridges. Although there are over 40 different species of quail in the world, the number of species kept domestically or commercially is quite small. The book concentrates on the breeding and management of those species, notably the Coturnix laying strains and the ornamental aviary breeds.

I am very grateful to Mark of *Quails from Wales* who has supplied many photographs of his birds, and also to *Poultry World* magazine for allowing me to use some of their photographs of commercial units.

The book is primarily a practical book based on my own experiences of keeping quail. I hope that quail breeders, producers, hobbyists, schools and agricultural colleges, and indeed anyone interested in these fascinating little birds will find something of interest within these pages.

Katie Thear, Newport, 2005

A pair of the author's Coturnix laying quail.

History of the quail

There went forth a wind from the Lord and brought quails from the sea.
(Exodus)

The earliest known representation of the quail is in Egyptian hieroglyph-ics, when the little bird was common enough and important enough to merit a place in the alphabet. Carvings of the period indicate that it was caught in nets, along with other species, and represented an important part of the diet. In China, too it was represented in carvings and ceramics.

There are two closely related species in the wild, the Common or Euro-pean quail, *Coturnix coturnix*, and the Eurasian or Pharoah quail, *Coturnix communis*. The chances are that they are derived from a common source. The Japanese quail, *Coturnix coturnix japonica*, has been bred from the wild form and is heavier. Its pedigree dates back to the 12th century when it was valued as a songbird. Most farmed quail are based on Japanese strains.

Stone Age man was apparently partial to quail meat! Remains of Coturnix quail have been found in early Upper Pleistocene rocks in Britain, notably in Chudleigh Cave and Kent's Cave in Devon, Hoe Grange Cave in Derby-shire and Kirkdale Cave in Yorkshire.

They make their appearance, too, in the literature, art and music of dif-ferent periods. In the Bible, there is reference to how food was brought to the starving Israelites in the wilderness, as shown by the quotation at the top of the page. The Israelites feeding on quail are also depicted in an 11th century Spanish manuscript (Vatican Library), as well as in the *Rohan Book of Hours*. The *Sherborne Missal* of 1400 has a good representation of a quail, while the *Pilkington Charter* (Fitzwilliam Museum, Cambridge) depicts a somewhat obscure one which could arguably be a partridge! The late 14th century English poem, *Pearl*, describes the quail's propensity for keeping still in face of danger: *"I stod as stylle as a dased quayle."*

Coturnix quail were kept as aviary and fighting birds by the early Greeks. The island of Ortygia (the ancient name for Delos) is derived from the Greek name *ortyx* for quail. Dionysius and Aristotle refer to them, as well as the Roman writer Pliny who said that their flocks were hazardous to shipping! Varro thought highly of them as a source of profit: *"Other birds fetch a good price, such as ortolans and quails."*

Shakespeare refers to the ancient practice of quail fighting in *Antony and Cleopatra*, when Antony bemoans the fact that Caesar's chances of winning are greater than his: *"His cocks do win the battle still of mine when it is all to naught and his quails ever beat mine, inhooped at odds."*

Early Representations of Quail

Relief from the temple
of Seti 1 at Abydos.

Painted relief from the tomb of
Seti1 at Thebes.

Section of the Hunefor
papyrus scroll.

The quail in the
hieroglyphic
alphabet - 'ut'

Right:
From *The Transnotation of Bird Voices*
by Athanasias Kircher, 1650.

Woodcut from *Mrs Beeton's Book of
Household Management*, 1861.

Woodcut from Thomas Bewick's
History of Birds, 1820

Shakespeare also uses the term quail as a reference to a prostitute, while in the USA, a 'San Quentin quail' is possibly of the same ilk. In Egypt the term quail is used to describe someone well fed. It was also commonly used as a dimunitive and familiar term of affection, as Donna Woolfolk Cross demonstrates in her novel about the 9th century, *Pope Joan: "Trust me, little quail."*

Beethoven utilizes the call of the quail in his music. See if you can spot it in the *Pastoral Symphony!* Leopald Mozart (father of Amadeus) also includes the quail in the *Toy Symphony*, while Althanasias Kircher produced a written notation for the quail's song in 1650!

The seventeenth century East Anglian poet, John Clare, could recognise the quail on a summer's evening: *"While in the juicy corn the hidden quail cries 'wet my foot' and hid as thoughts unborn."* As a true countryman, he did not confuse it with the similar looking but larger corncrake, which, *"utters 'craik, craik' like voices underground."*

Gilbert White, eighteenth century vicar of Selborne and author of *The Natural History of Selborne,* makes several references to quail. He records hearing their calls between June 22nd and July 8th, 1774. In 1786, the calls were apparently emanating from *"the field next to the garden"*, while in 1787, the first call of the year was on May 20th *"at Rolle"*.

In 1820, Thomas Bewick illustrated the quail in his *History of Birds,* while, 1891 saw them in another classic; Morris's *British Birds.* In 1859, Mrs. Beeton wrote: *"Quails are almost universally diffused over Europe, Asia and Africa, in the autumn, and returning again in the spring, frequently alighting in their passage on many of the islands of the Archipelago, which, with their vast numbers, they almost completely cover. It appears highly probable that the quails which supplied the Israelites with food during their journey through the wilderness, were sent by a wind from the southwest, sweeping over Egypt towards the shores of the Red Sea. In England they are not very numerous, although they breed and many of them are said to remain throughout the year, changing their quarters from the interior parts of the country for the seacoast."* (It is unclear whether she is referring to the British Isles, or only to England - the latter being a frequent misnomer for Wales, Scotland and Ireland!)

Sir Herbert Maxwell wrote: *"The fecundity of the species must be prodigious, millions being taken in nets during their spring and autumn migrations across the Mediterranean."*

The effects of intensive farming have been to reduce the numbers of wild Coturnix quail which arrive in Britain. At one time, they were widespread as summer visitors. Now, they are rare immigrants arriving between May and July from Africa, via the Mediterranean and Northern Europe. In 'good' years they are to be found in some cereal and hay fields in southern Britain.

The quail's retiring habit has given rise to the verb *to quail*. The Reverend Patrick Bronte makes use of it in a letter to Ellen Hussey in 1885, when he refers to Mrs Gaskell's undertaking to write the life of his daughter Charlotte: *"No quailing, Mrs Gaskell! No drawing back!"*

In recent years, a considerable Coturnix quail industry has grown in the United States, Japan, Italy, France and Britain. This is to cater for the gourmet interest in quails' eggs and delicatessen table birds. In many countries, it also has the dubious distinction of being bred for laboratory testing.

Worldwide, there are thirteen sub-groupings of quail but compared with the total number of quail breeds in the world, only a small number are kept and bred domestically. *The Quail Group* of the *World Pheasant Association* monitors the situation. The next chapter gives details of the different types and how they relate to each other.

The Bobwhite quail is kept as a farmed table bird in some areas of the USA, and also as a 'managed habitat bird' for the hunting sector, in a similar way to that of pheasant rearing in the United Kingdom.

The Chinese Painted, *Coturnix chinensis* is widely kept as an aviary bird. Traditionally it has been kept as a ground clearer when flying birds such as finches and doves spill seeds on the aviary floor. In recent years, with the growing popularity of butterfly houses, it has also gained the role of a spider catcher, to prevent butterflies being caught in the webs. (It should be added that Chinese Painted quail need to be given a daily ration of food, for the spillings of other birds cannot be regarded as a proper diet).

There have been many references to quails, but perhaps the last word should go to a schoolboy who sent me the following poem about the quail, and which I was pleased to include in the first edition. I don't think that any of the writers of ancient civilizations have bettered his description:

Short and plump,
Timid but inquisitive,
Dull but pretty,
Not very clever,
But a long way from silly.
(Alex Smith)

Common quail, *Coturnix coturnix.*
British Birds - Morris. 1891

About the quail

We loathe our manna and we long for quails.
(Dryden, 1682)

Classification

If we 'place' quail in their relative position in the bird world, they are found in the order of *Galliformes*. This is a group that includes game birds and domestic fowl, but not waterfowl. Narrowing the classification further, it is a member of the *Phasiandae* family, a category it shares with pheasants and partridges.

Class: AVES (Birds)
Order: GALLIFORMES (Game birds and Fowl)
Family: PHASIANIDAE (Pheasants, Partridges and Quail)
Genus: Quail (13 different genera as follows)

- Anurophasis
- Callipepla
- Colinus
- Cotumix
- Cyrtonyx
- Dactylortyx
- Dendrortyx
- Odontophorus
- Ophrysia
- Oreortyx
- Perdicula
- Philortyx
- Rhynchortyx

The most widely kept quail are the *Coturnix* laying varieties, some of the *Colinus* group, such as the Bobwhite, and the small aviary Chinese Painted quail which is also a member of the Coturnix genus.

Most quails are birds of the undergrowth which, depending on the area, may be tall grasses, dense bush, shrub thickets, overgrown fields, meadows, plantations or savannahs. They are essentially shy, retiring birds which will 'quail' with fear into the shadow and security of the undergrowth. They stand motionless. When really disturbed however, they will break cover like pheasants, flying straight up in the air with a characteristic whirring of wings.

Ground orientation and camouflage

Most are ground-orientated in that they spend most of their time on the ground in the wild, except when they are migrating or disturbed in some way. Some are more ground orientated than others. The Chinese Painted, for example, is like a small mouse scuttling about on the ground, resorting to occasional short flights where necessary. The Bobwhite, by comparison, likes to fly and perch, and does not scratch as much as Coturnix. It is important, therefore, to make provision for such behaviour within an aviary.

Quail Groups
including Old and New World Genera

Anurophasis
Snow Mountain quail, *A. monorthoryx*

Callipepla
Californian quail, *Callipepla californica*
Elegant quail, *Callipepla douglasii*
Gambel's quail, *Callipepla gambelii*
Scaled quail, *Callipepla squamata*

Colinus
Crested Bobwhite quail, *Colinus cristatus*
Blackthroated Bobwhite, *C. nigrogularis*
Bobwhite quail, *Colinus virginianus*

Coturnix
Common/European quail, *C. coturnix*
Eurasian/Pharaoh quail, *C. c. communis*
Japanese quail, *Coturnix c. japonica*
Harlequin quail, *Coturnix delegorguei*
Asian Blue (Chinese Painted /Blue
Breasted, King) *Coturnix c. chinensis*
African Blue quail, *Coturnix adansonii*
Rain quail, *Coturnix coromandelica*
Grey (Stubble, Pectoral) quail, *Coturnix pectoralis*
New Zealand quail, *C. novaezeelandiae* (extinct)
Brown (Swamp) quail, *C. ypsilophorus*

Cyrtonyx
Mearns quail, *Cyrtonyx montezumae*
Ocellated quail, *Cyrtonyx ocellatus*

Dactylortyx
Singing quail, *Dactylortyx thoracicus*

Dendrortyx
Bearded Tree quail, *Dendrortyx barbatus*
Buffycrowned Tree quail, *D. leucophys*
Longtailed Tree quail, *D. macroura*

Odontophorus
Blackfronted Wood quail, *O. atrifrons*
Stripefaced Wood quail, *O. balliviani*
Spotwinged Wood quail, *O. capueira*
Venezuelan Wood quail, *O. columbianus*

Tacarcuna Wood quail, *O. dialucos*
Rufous-fronted Wood quail, *O. erythrops*
Rufous-breasted Wood quail, *O. speciosus*
Marbled Wood quail, *O. gujanensis*
Spotted Wood quail, *O. guttatus*
Chestnut Wood quail, *O. hyperythrus*
Whitethroated (Blackbreasted) Wood
quail, *Odontophorus leucolaemus*
Darkbacked Wood quail, *O. melanonotus*
Starred Wood quail, *O. stellatus*
Gorgeted Wood quail, *O. strophium*

Ophrysia
Indian Mountain (Himalayan) quail,
Ophrysia superciliosa

Oreotyx
Mountain quail, *Oreotyx pictus*

Perdicula
Rock Bush quail, *Perdicula argoondah*
Jungle Bush quail, *Perdicula asiatica*
Painted Bush quail, *P. erythrorhyncha*
Manipur Bush quail, *P. manipurensis*

Philortyx
Banded quail, *Philortyx fasciatus*

Rhynchortyx
Tawny faced quail, *Rhynchortyx cinctus*

Recent DNA findings have established
that Button quail are not true quail, but
are members of the unrelated order of
Turniciformes.
The Chinese Painted quail, mistakenly
called Button quail, especially in the USA,
are true quail - *Coturnix coturnix chinensis*.

*Where names are shown in brackets,
this indicates alternatively used names*

Characteristics of Coturnix quail

Sharp beak for picking up grains and insects

Upright flight take-off to escape ground predators

Sharp eyesight provides protection against predators such as hawks and crows

Stippled feather markings provide camouflage in long grass and undergrowth

Strong claws to scratch soil to reveal insects

Ability to 'quail' motionlessly and avoid being seen

Clumps of grass or shrubs are needed to provide cover, with a couple of branches for perching.

The stippling effect on the plumage provides good camouflage. The lines blend in with those of tall grasses, so clumps of vegetation in the aviary are well received. I once dropped a Japanese quail outside when I was transferring him into an outside grazing pen. He immediately disappeared into some tall grasses near a copse of trees. Despite a search, I never found him, yet he could have been just a few feet away. I like to think that he joined up with some migratory wild quail, but the chances are that he fell foul of the many shooters in the area.

Upward flight

As referred to earlier, Coturnix quail fly straight upwards when disturbed, in the same way that pheasants break cover. In the wild, this is a useful manoeuvre to escape from predators, although it exposes them to those who are out shooting. In housed conditions the same pattern is also to be found. The birds have a tendency to fly straight up and dash their heads on the roof, sometimes causing injury. It is apparent all through the year, but much more so in the period leading up to the breeding season when the migratory urge is at its peak. The only way to deal with this in an aviary or roofed run is to stretch some soft netting just below the solid roof so that they do not hurt themselves.

Toes and claws

Most breeds of quail have long toes and claws, an adaptation for scratching for insectivorous foods. In an aviary there is usually provision for this, but if there is only a concrete run, do make sure they have an area where fine soil,

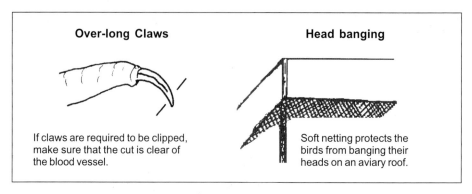

Over-long Claws	**Head banging**
If claws are required to be clipped, make sure that the cut is clear of the blood vessel.	Soft netting protects the birds from banging their heads on an aviary roof.

sand or wood shavings can be made available. The Bobwhite's strong claws are particularly adapted for perching and a hard flat surface is inappropriate, although acceptable for Chinese Painted quail.

Scratching conditions are vital for Coturnix breeds, not only to cater for their instinctive need to scratch, but also to keep the claws in trim. In housed conditions it may be necessary to cut them. Hold the bird gently in one hand, using the fingers to keep the limb steady, then clip the claws with nail clippers. Do this in a good light so that you can see where the blood vessel within the claw ends, so that the cut is made beyond it. It is painless, and nail clippers can be used.

The beak

The quail's beak is long, pointed and sharp, ideally suited for pecking small insects and grains, or for shredding small pieces of vegetation. It can also be an aggressive weapon if one quail decides to attack another. The males will fight to the extent that they cause considerable damage. In some intensive units, quails are beak trimmed; the upper beak is trimmed back so that it is shorter than the lower one, but I find such a practice repugnant. Another practice, more common in the USA than in Britain, is to use beak rings. These are open rings which have the ends inserted into the nostrils and then pinched together with pliers. Again, I abhor such a practice.

In the wild, the beak is kept relatively short by access to a range of natural materials. In captivity it is a good idea to provide a dried cuttlefish bone for this purpose, as is commonly done for canaries and budgerigars. Most pet shops sell it. Make sure that it is positioned firmly so that there is adequate friction when the beak is rubbed against it.

Calls

The question is often asked - how noisy are quail? As with all things, only a relative answer is possible. As a generalisation, males are noisier than fe-

The stippled markings of the feathers help to provide camouflage in the wild.

males which confine themselves to subdued little chirrups and soft 'tic-tics' or cooings. The male Coturnix has a rasping chirrupping crow, rather like the harsh cry of the magpie, and is altogether louder and more penetrating. Traditionally, this has been described as sounding like 'wet-my-lips' or 'wet-my-feet'. Athanasias Kircher, in 1650, decided that it was saying 'bik-e-bik', and produced a musical notation to illustrate it (See page 6).

The photograph on page 14 shows a Tuxedo Coturnix male adopting the characteristic upright stance and open-beaked expression when letting the world know of his whereabouts. This uptight stance is also the one that was depicted in the Egyptian hieroglyphics.

The Bobwhite male is also loud, but I do not find his call as aggravating as that of the Coturnix. It is basically a three-note, full-bodied piping, whistling sound. The female has a quieter version of the same call, with more of a tendency to chirrup.

The Chinese Painted male has a melodious, rather wistful piping whistle. It is almost minor-key, with an evocative atmosphere of the jungle in it. The female is quiet, apart from the occasional and busy 'chic-chic' as she darts about looking for insects.

Preening

Like all birds, quails will preen themselves regularly, often standing in a patch of sunlight to do so. This ritual of cleaning the feathers with the beak

Three Common Postures of Coturnix Quail

'Quailing' into the grass to avoid being detected. This is a normal Coturnix layer.

Normal 'at ease' posture shown by this Fawn Coturnix.

Upright posture when calling. This Tuxedo has the same pose as that shown in Egyptian hieroglyphics.

also allows a certain amount of waterproofing to take place. It is also a sign that the bird is healthy. A quail which does not preen itself, but has a tendency to stand, looking morose, should be checked, because it is a sign that all is not well. They will also take baths, given the opportunity to do so, as the photograph on page 31 shows.

Size
Quail vary in size, from the largest Longtailed Tree quail, *Dendrortyx macroura*, at 36 cm (14 in), to the smallest Chinese Painted quail, *Coturnix coturnix chinensis* at 12 cm (4.5 in). They are found in a wide range of climates, but all share similar characteristics of being shy, quick and with a tendency to hide in ground cover such as long grass or other vegetation.

Life span
There is little information available on this aspect, but Altman and Ditmer, in their report, *Growth including Reproduction and Morphological Development*, 1962 (USA), say that the record life span of a Coturnix quail is ten years. Commercially, it is between 1-2 years.

Taming
As a general rule, males should be kept separate to avoid fighting and interbreeding, but on a small scale, where there is less pressure of numbers and general stress, they may live together quite happily without fighting. On a small scale birds do become tame. I frequently allowed up to seven different males to share the same aviary and run in the summer, with occasional

Quail can become tame. This British Range often sat on the author's conservatory table when she was working. Note the large feet in comparison with its size, an adaptation for scratching.

browsing periods on grass in a moveable run. In winter, they were housed in canary or parrot breeding cages in the conservatory, but were frequently released to enjoy the freedom of the conservatory.

I did not let the breeds interbreed, of course. When I wanted to collect eggs for incubation purposes, I confined the male and females of a particular breed together and kept them separate from the others until I could be sure that the eggs were pure.

I must emphasize that my birds were probably demonstrating behaviour different from the norm, because they were so tame. On sunny winter days, I often worked at a table in the conservatory. One or more of the quail would fly up and see what I was up to, often settling down and going to sleep a few inches away.

As a matter of interest, there is an American book called *That Quail Robert* by Margaret Stranger which is a fascinating account of how the author tamed a Bobwhite quail.

Coturnix quail

Normal Coturnix laying quail in a grassed aviary.

This is the most common type in captivity worldwide. It is essentially the same bird that the Ancient Egyptians knew and that Mrs. Beeton would have recognised as one of the *'feathered game which have from time immemorial given gratification to the palate of man"*. When reference is made to quail in general, this is the bird in question.

There is a great deal of confusion about the origin of Coturnix quail as we know them today, so it is appropriate to consider how their development took place. Part of the confusion undoubtedly lies in the fact that there are so many different local names, as well as old scientific names now replaced by modern classifications. In the table opposite these are all in brackets.

Development of Coturnix quail

No-one can know for certain how the various breeds and sub-species developed, but it is generally acknowledged that all the Coturnix types are originally based on the Common quail, *Coturnix coturnix*, the wild migratory bird of Europe, Asia and Africa. Various sub-species developed from this, including the European quail, *Coturnix coturnix coturnix*, the Eurasian quail,

Coturnix coturnix communis, and the Japanese quail, *Coturnix coturnix japonica.* Also associated with the Common quail are the Stubble quail, *Coturnix pectoralis,* and the Brown quail, *Coturnix ypsilophorus,* of Australia. In India there is the Rain quail, *Coturnix coromendelia,* while Africa has the Harlequin quail, *Coturnix delegorguei.* New Zealand once had its own variety of New Zealand quail, *Coturnix novaezelandicae,* but this is now extinct.

The Asian Blue and the African Blue are smaller members of the Coturnix family. These, like their larger cousins are now to be found in various subspecies and colour variations. These are indicated later.

Coturnix laying quail

I use the term normal type Coturnix to indicate those birds that are normally kept commercially for the production of eggs or for the table. It also differentiates them from those Coturnix breeds that are kept as ornamentals, such as the Asian Blue.

The Japanese quail is the basis for most of the commercial quail that are now kept. It was first recognised in the nineteenth century as a separate breed in the wild, although it had been bred by the Japanese as a singing bird as early as the 12th century. In recent years, Japanese quail have been developed in more productive commercial strains, as well as for use in the laboratory. The Eurasian or Pharoah quail, *Coturnix coturnix communis,* has

also contributed to the development of commercial strains in the USA. Coturnix breeds are often referred to as *Old World Quail* because they were introduced by European settlers, and it distinguishes them from indigenous *New World Quail* such as the Bobwhite. These introductions had numerous names, including Pharoah, Bible, Nile, Tsar, King, Mediterranean or German.

The normal type male Coturnix grows to around 16cm (6.5in), while the female is slightly larger at an average of 18cm (7.5in). Both sexes have dappled dark brown buff and cream striated backs, paler underbellies, breast and flanks. In the female, the markings are less pronounced, while the male's chest is reddish brown. This particular feature enables sex identification to take place from 3 weeks of age. Before then, it is difficult to do so. In both sexes there is a distinctive light stripe above the eye, and a white collar, although this may be diminished in the female. The beak is yellow-brown to dark olive-brown, the legs pinkish yellow and the eyes dark brown. This description refers to the normal Coturnix laying quail. There are also varieties that differ in colour and markings.

Normal Laying Coturnix (male) in a grass run. The board at the side provides protection against the wind.

Commercial strains

Different names have been given to strains that have been developed through selection. Those that are reared for commercial purposes include:

Jumbo This is a table strain developed for increased size and weight, although the colour and markings are the same as those of the normal type.

Spanish This is a smaller bird bred for egg production. It was given this name by the distributor who introduced it from France, to differentiate between it and other French strains. Colour and markings are the same as the normal type. There are also colour variations.

Italian Also called the Golden Italian, it has become popular as a layer.

Colour varieties

Gold

As just referred to, this is essentially the same breed as other strains of Coturnix laying quail, but has been developed as a separate variety with golden colouring. The male is lighter while the female is darker and more striated. She also has distinctive brown stripes around the face.

The gene for gold colouring is dominant.

Golden Italian Coturnix with distinctive head markings of the female.

Thus, a Gold crossed with a normal Coturnix type will produce mainly gold young, and a few brown feathered ones, in the ratio of 2:1. It is worth bearing in mind that two doses of the gold gene are associated with a lethal condition, with up to 25% of the eggs failing to hatch.

In the USA, golden strains known as **Manchurian Gold** were developed by Marsh Farms. Various Golds there have been bred for the table and eggs. In Britain and Europe, **Italian** or **Golden Italian** is the name given to the golden variety. This is slightly smaller than the normal type and is kept predominantly as an egg layer. It should be added that with Italian, and indeed with any other strain of Coturnix quail, too much in-breeding is to be avoided. An infusion of fresh blood, with a system of careful breeding and up-grading (bearing in mind the comments about lethal gene combinations) would be a positive step. (See also page 73).

Range

The overall colouring is dark brown, so that some people refer to them as Brown quail. This is a mistake however, for the Brown quail is the name normally given to the Australian breed which is bigger and more greyish in appearance. However, there is a similarity and it is possible that Australian settlers introduced the Common quail to that Continent, with subsequent isolated development producing apparently different sub-species. The markings of the Range are essentially a lighter brown body colour overlaid with

White Coturnix hen in a moveable run on grass.

darker-brown, almost black pencilling, along with a certain amount of dark grey feathering on the back and as a faint patch on the throat. In America, the Range Coturnix, is referred to as the **British Range**, while in the UK, we sometimes call it the **American Range**!

The overall appearance is dark-brown while the striped head markings are similar to other Coturnix breeds. However, the white eyebrow stripe and white throat markings are virtually absent. Beak and legs are olive-brown and eyes, dark brown. The brown plumage is the result of a dominant gene.

Fawn Coturnix. *(Quails from Wales)*

Fawn

This is one of my favourites. Essentially like all the other Coturnix breeds, the overall impression of the Fawn is a lovely warm pinkish-brown. The fawn feathers are pencilled with white and the white eyebrow lines are present, although not as strongly defined as in other breeds. Beak and legs are light pinkish-brown, and eyes are dark brown.

There is no colour difference between the sexes, although as in other breeds, the female is slightly bigger than the male. In the USA, there is a similar variety called the **American Fawn** or the **American Spotted Fawn**.

White

Sometimes called **English White**, good specimens are completely white, with no discernible markings, other than the merest hint of eyebrow lines

on the head. Beak and legs are pinkish brown and eyes are dark brown. Male and female are identical, although the female is larger. It is common to have patches of black on the head and back. Breeders who are aiming for all-white specimens can breed this out with careful selective breeding, but beware! White is regarded as a recessive gene, but in recent years, an incompletely dominant albino gene has also been reported. So, it is important to remember that too much emphasis on trying to produce an all-white bird may produce unwanted albinos.

Tuxedo

This is an apt name for a bird with a smart white waistcoat to contrast with its dark brown overcoat. The two-colour pied pattern is the result of a crossing between the dominant dark brown and recessive white genes.

The colour of the back feathers is identical with those of the Range, while the white plumage is like that of the English White. The markings are often variable. The ideal ones are clear white face, chest and belly, with dark brown back, tail and crown. In good specimens, the brown and white feathering is neatly demarcated, but it is common to find patches of white where the brown should be, and vice versa.

Other colours

In recent years, crossings and mutations have also produced a range of varying colours, hues and feather patterning, including Cream, Grey, Blue, Grey/Blue, Ginger, Red, and so on. It is important to remember that these strains are all variations of the basic type of Coturnix or Japanese Laying quail, and not separate breeds. On page 73, the known genetic factors, both dominant and recessive are indicated.

A group of Chinese Painted quail. *(Quails from Wales).*

Aviary Coturnix breeds

In addition to the normal and coloured varieties of Coturnix laying quail, there are other Coturnix breeds that are often kept as aviary birds, rather than as producers.

Chinese Painted quail

The Chinese Painted, Asian Blue, King, or Blue Breasted quail, *Coturnix coturnix chinensis*, is the smallest of the quail breeds, with the male reaching 12cm (4.5in) and the female 13cm (5in). In appearance it is compact and round, with a mouse-like way of scuttling about. The male is far more colourful than the female, with a brown and blue flecked back and crown. Breast and tail feathers are reddish brown, while the chin and throat have distinct black and white striping, like a smart crescent collar. The female is less flamboyant, with an overall mottled brownish hue from the fine black and white specks. Her back is slightly darker than her abdomen. She has a white patch on the throat but no barring. In both sexes the beak is black and the eyes are brown. The Chinese Painted quail is probably the most widely kept of the ornamental aviary breeds. It is arguably the prettiest and most colourful, and in recent years has been much utilised as a spider catcher in butterfly houses. Anyone who has ever visited one of the increasing number of butterfly breeding establishments, such as that at Syon Park in Middlesex, will have seen these busy little birds scuttling through the ground vegetation of the greenhouses, beady eyes on the lookout for unwary spiders.

Button quail are not true quail

Unlike true quail, the Button quail has no hind toe. The male is less colourful than the female and he does the work of incubating the eggs.

Chinese Painted quail - a true quail of the Coturnix family.

Button quail - a hemipode of the Turnix family.

Found in China, India, Sri-Lanka, South Africa and Australia, there are around ten sub-species of the Chinese Painted. They are all similar but with slight variations. Many are now rare. They include the following:

African Painted quail or Blue quail, *Coturnix chinensis adansonii*. The male is darker backed, but the wings are striped reddish brown and grey.

Australian or Eastern King quail, *Coturnix chinensis lineata*. This has more distinct lines on the plumage, hence the *lineata* designation.

Other sub-species are *C. c. trinkutansis, C. c. colletti, C. c. papuensis, C. c. lepida* and *C. c. novaeguinea* from New Guinea.

Colour varieties of Chinese Painted quail

In recent years, there has been a considerable amount of breeding to produce different colour varieties. These are all variations of the Asian Blue Chinese Painted, which is the most commonly found. These varieties are either called by the colour itself, or referred to as 'coloured' or mutation', eg, Blue, Blue Coloured, or Blue Mutation.

Silver: This is the most common mutation and has all the feathers in varying shades of light pastel grey. It first appeared as a natural mutation in the UK , in the 1940s.

White: These are all-white, although not albinos. There may be a few coloured feathers in some birds, but the aim is to produce a snow white effect.

Red-breasted: The face is almost black with a fine white line around the eye. The red area extends from the vent, across the breast to the throat.

Red Breasted Silver: Here the pastel grey plumage contrasts beautifully with the pinkish red breast.

Fawn or Cinnamon: Developed in Australia, this is called Fawn in Europe

Harlequin hen. (*Quails from Wales*).

and Cinnamon in the USA, although differences are now being developed, eg, the Fawn is slightly darker. There is also a Blue-Faced and a Red-Breasted Fawn, as well as a Smoky version.

Blue: The plumage is a dark, overall blue-grey.

Black: This is an even darker blue-grey, approaching black.

Ivory: Lighter than Silver, it has an overall ivory hue, and the male's breast is grey.

Golden Pearl: Originating in Europe, this has yellow feathering with light brown barring. There is also a Fawn or Cinnamon Pearl, and a Blue-Faced Pearl. No doubt there will continue to be other colour variations produced.

When is a Button not a Button?

The answer to this question is - when it's a Turnix. The Americans have quite wrongly given the name Button quail to Chinese Painted quail. When American servicemen first saw Chinese Painteds in European aviaries, they described them as being 'as cute as a button'. When the birds were then introduced to the USA, the name stuck. So, when Americans refer to Button quail, they really mean Chinese Painteds!

Button quail are not quail at all! They are hemipodes (from the Greek meaning half foot because they do not have a hind toe). They belong to the *Turnicidae* family and are more related to rails and cranes than to quails.

Several types of Button quail are found in Africa and India, including the Barred Button quail, *Turnix suscitator*, and the Yellow-Legged Button quail, *Turnix tanki*. There is also a very rare Andalusian hemipode, *Turnix sylvatica*, in the Andalucia region of Spain.

Harlequin quail

The Harlequin quail, *Coturnix delegorguei*, is from central to southern Africa. It is sometimes confused with Mearns (Montezuma) quail, *Cyrtonyx montezumae*, because the latter also has the common name Harlequin. However, there is no connection between the two for Mearns is a New World quail from Central America.

The plumage is brown with lighter striations and there is an eye stripe in both sexes. The male also has a distinctive face mask which is absent in the female. The breed is found in aviaries, including those in the UK.

Rain quail

Also found in UK aviaries, the Rain quail, *Coturnix coromandelica*, comes from India. The breed is sometimes called the Black Breasted quail because the male's breast is a dark contrast to the rest of the brown plumage. This is absent in the female, as are the prominent facial markings.

Grey quail

Alternative names for this are Stubble, Pectoral or Australian quail, the latter indicating that it is found in Australia. *Coturnix pectoralis* is also an aviary bird there, although rarely found elsewhere. It is similar to normal Coturnix laying quail but the male has more red colouring on the head, chin and breast.

Brown quail

Also from Australia is the Brown quail, *Coturnix ypsilophorus*. Other names by which it is called are Swamp, Silver or Tasmanian. It was originally given the scientific name, *Synoicus ypsilophorus*, but more modern nomenclature now refers to it as *Coturnix ypsilophorus*.

The breed is similar to the normal Coturnix laying quail, but the female can be distinguished by more prominent black stripes on her underparts.

There was, at one time, a New Zealand quail, *Coturnix novaezelandicae*, with the common name of Koreke, but this is now thought to be extinct.

Other Aviary Breeds

Hail with shrill whistle the note of the quail,
the bobwhite dodging by bay-bush. (T.S. Elliot)

Common Bobwhite showing the characteristic face mask of the male..

There are many breeds of quail that are not from the Coturnix family, in different parts of the world, but relatively few are kept in captivity. Some of those most likely to be found in UK aviaries are listed here. For details of other breeds, there is an excellent, large-format book called *The Atlas of Quails* by David Alderton, published by *T.F.H. Publications.*

Bobwhite

The Common Bobwhite quail, *Colinus virginianus,* is a breed which has its distribution mainly in North and Central America, although its indigenous habitat is east of the Rockies in mid-west and southern USA. Alternative names are American quail, Northern Bobwhite and Partridge Quail. The latter name is an appropriate one for they are more like partridges than quail.

In the USA the Bobwhite is primarily regarded as a 'managed habitat game bird' for the benefit of hunters. Where it is raised for meat, the Eastern variety of Bobwhite is heavier and more suitable. There are over twenty sub-species of the breed. It is a bigger bird altogether than the Coturnix layer, with the male reaching 25cm (9.5in) and female 27cm (10.5in). By comparison with other game birds, however, it is relatively small. The back, tail and crown of both sexes are dark brown, while the chest, belly and flanks are lighter, with black and white striations. A white stripe covers the eyebrows and, in the male, there is a white patch under the chin. In some females, this patch is absent or reduced, being replaced by buff markings. The overall colour effect is less bright in the female.

The beak is greyish-brown, legs yellowish-brown and eyes dark brown. The Bobwhite is a most attractive bird. I kept a pair in an aviary and they proved to be easy to tame as I have already mentioned. They have a greater tendency to fly and perch than other breeds of quail, so they really need perching facilities.

Colour varieties of Bobwhite
Natural mutations and subsequent crossings have produced several colour varieties of the Bobwhite. They include: Black, White, Pied, Speckled, Red, Silver, Chestnut and Fawn. No doubt there will be more.

Mearns quail
The alternative name for this Central American breed is Montezuma quail, *Cyrtonyx montezumae*, although in some parts of the USA they also give it the common name of Harlequin quail. This causes confusion between it and the old world *Coturnix delegorguei*, the true Harlequin quail.

The female is light brown with whitish areas on the face and on the tips of the back feathers. The male is much grander, with white spots on bluish-grey sides and abdomen, and brown and black back and wings. He also has a black and white face and a chestnut crown. Mearns quails are best kept in pairs for the females have been known to fight each other.

Californian quail
Also called Valley quail, the state bird of California, *Callipepla californica* is an attractive bird with a forward-pointing crest which is present in both sexes but is shorter in the female. The breed is quite common in aviaries but I was also lucky enough to see some wild ones on the edge of Lake Cachuma in California. Both sexes are brown and fawn but the male has a bluish-grey front and a dark face with white stripe.

Californian quail
(Clipart Collection)

28

Mearns hen. *(Quails from Wales)*

Blue Scaled quail

The Blue Scaled quail, *Callipepla squamata*, is also called the Scaled quail. The former is an apt description of its distinctive blue-grey front feathering with their delicate scale markings. It comes from the desert areas of Central America and there are several sub-species, including the Chestnut Bellied Blue Scale and the Arizona Scaled quail.

Both sexes have tufted crests and look alike, although the female's crest is more buff coloured than that of the male. The male also has a plain chin while that of the female is slightly striped. They are said to be very vocal birds.

Mountain quail

The Mountain quail, *Oreortyx pictus*, comes from the west coast of North America and is another breed with a spectacular crest that is found in both sexes, although that of the female is shorter. Interestingly, the long narrow crest is composed of only two feathers.

The chest, head and back are bluish-grey while the face and neck are chestnut bordered by a white stripe. The abdomen is striped black and white and the lower back and wings are brown.

Alternative names are Plumed quail and Painted quail, although the latter is another source of confusion, this time with the little Chinese Painted.

Relative Sizes of Quail

Breed	Length
Normal Japanese quail	15 - 18 cm (6 - 7 in)
Jumbo Japanese quail	18 - 20 cm (7 - 8 in)
Italian Laying quail	13 - 15 cm (5 - 6 in)
Spanish Laying quail	13 - 15 cm (5 - 6 in)
Blue Scaled quail	24 - 27 cm (9.5 - 10.5 in)
Bobwhite quail	24 - 27 cm (9.5 - 10.5 in)
Californian quail	24 - 27 cm (9.5 - 10.5 in)
Chinese Painted quail	11 - 13 cm (4.5 - 5 in)
Gambel's quail	24 - 27 cm (9.5 - 10.5 in)
Harlequin quail	16.5 - 18 cm (6.5 - 7 in)
Mearns quail	20 - 23 cm (8 - 9 in)
Mountain quail	27 - 29 cm (10.5 - 11.5in)

Please note that these are average sizes only, with the female being slightly larger than the male in many cases.

Gambel's quail

Named after a nineteenth century American naturalist, William Gambel, the Gambel's quail, *Callipepla gambelii*, is from the south-west of the USA. Both sexes have a plumed crest, often called the top-knot and similar to that of the Californian quail, although again, the female's crest is shorter.

The plumage of both sexes is brownish grey on top and buff underneath, while the sides are reddish brown with a white streak. The male is easily distinguished by its dark face outlined in white and the darker area on its abdomen.

Male Rain quail in an aviary. *(Quails from Wales)*.

Quail spend a lot of time preening and grooming their feathers. They will also take baths if given the chance. This one is shaking itself dry after bathing.

The distinctive eye stripe is common to both sexes of Coturnix quail, although in light varieties such as the White it is masked by the colour. This one is a Fawn Coturnix.

Commercial egg laying quail in a cage system. Note how the eggs roll into a collecting area at the front. *(Poultry World)*.

Housing

Less stereotypic behaviour is seen in floor pens than in cages.

(Code of Practice for Housing & Care of Animals in Designated Breeding Establishhments. 10: Quail. Home Office).

Quails are fairly small birds and their needs are modest, but they still need proper housing. Whatever form it takes, it must provide shelter from the elements and predators, adequate warmth and ventilation, and a clean, hygienic environment. It's worth taking a look at the environmental requirements for adult quail. They can provide useful guidelines, bearing in mind that quail generally have originated from the more temperate areas of the world.

Temperature: 16 - 23ºC
Relative humidity: 30 - 80%

The system of housing depends very much on the type and scale of the quail enterprise, as well as on the type of quail being kept. A commercial system for Coturnix layers or table birds will obviously be more intensive than that where birds are kept primarily for interest. A small-scale enterprise may utilise small houses and runs. The more exotic breeds will usually be in aviaries, either indoor or outdoor, with attached house. Bobwhite quail, for example, must have aviary conditions with perching facilities. Whichever system is used, the salient point is that quails are not winter hardy and will need adequate housing.

Most commercial enterprises will use either a cage system or a floor-rearing one, or perhaps a combination of both. The former is where purpose-made cages, equipped with automatic watering facilities are used. The latter is where a building with a concrete floor is furnished with wood shavings, feeders and drinkers, and the birds can roam at will within the confines of the house. A concrete floor is essential, and the building needs to be substantial enough, not only to deter rodents but also to provide draught-free and well-ventilated, sheltered accommodation. Ventilation by roof ridge and side window is ideal, as a through current of fresh air is provided. The arrangement of this will vary depending on the type of house.

Lighting in a house is not only necessary for efficient managment, but it will also provide a stimulus for winter eggs, although table birds do not need extra light. Heating in winter is not necessary as long as there is enough insulation. Newly-hatched quail will naturally have localised heat in brooders until they are hardy. As there is so much variation in the types and scale of housing, it is a good idea to take a more detailed look at the options.

Varieties of Coturnix Laying Quail

Japanese male.

Pair of Italian quail. The male is at the back.

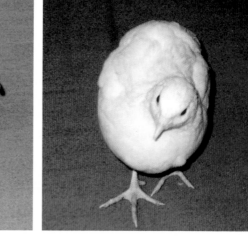

Range.

White.

(Photographs: Quails from Wales)

34

Dark Tuxedo

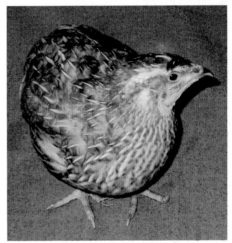

Fawn

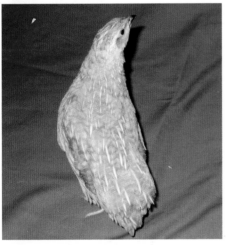

Platinum

Dark Chestnut

Grey Platinum Tuxedo

Cream

35

Cage systems

Cages, such as those shown on page 32, are used by most commercial units where eggs are being produced for sale. Some people, myself included, dislike cages on humanitarian grounds. There is no doubt that they make life easier for the producer, and egg collection is facilitated, but the birds' movements are restricted and foot problems are not uncommon. The use of flat welded mesh for the cage floors facilitates cleaning. It also prevents a possible build-up of disease, but does mean that the birds are unable to scratch in the way they do in unrestricted conditions.

'Deep-litter' type cages can also be used and these are favoured by many people because they provide a more natural flooring for the birds to scratch.

It is also possible to make your own cages, and welded mesh is suitable. Protective strip for the edges of cut welded mesh is available by the metre.

On a small scale, some people prefer to make their own cages using a wooden framework. Other alternatives are to adapt rabbit hutches or wooden bird breeding cages with solid wooden floors, sides and roofs, and a mesh cage front. These require a greater degree of management because the litter needs to be cleared out regularly.

Some of these wooden cages are often equipped with a sliding floor section so that cleaning is relatively simple. A section of weldmesh panel can also be inserted in one area of the floor to facilitate cleaning. I adapted a bank of rabbit hutches in this way and they worked well. The details are shown in the illustrations opposite.

It is important to bear in mind that, while most female birds can be housed together without any problems, some males will fight, sometimes to the death, and must be housed separately. Commercially, where sexes are reared together for the table, the light is kept low to delay the onset of sexual maturity, although growth continues.

Floor systems

A floor system is set up inside a building where the door has an interior flight entrance. This is essentially to stop birds escaping when you open the door, and works on the 'air-lock' principle. In other words, you close the outside door before opening the interior one. It need not necessarily be a door; it could be strips of wood or wire mesh strategically placed to provide a barrier. A floor system is also used for brooding young quail.

It must be emphasised, that quails can be great escapers and, as referred to earlier, can be impossible to locate once they get outside and find some natural cover.

Indoor rabbit hutches adapted for quail

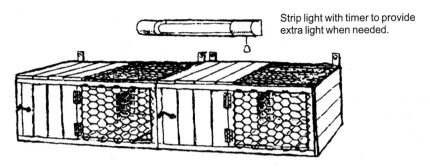

Strip light with timer to provide extra light when needed.

The covered areas provide sleeping accommodation while the wire mesh on the roof of the living area allows adequate light to enter to ensure winter egg production or to encourage early season breeding.

This system was used as winter housing only for the author's breeding birds. In the summer months they were in moveable runs on grass.

Wooden floor

Wooden wall of hutch

A droppings panel set into the floor of a wooden rabbit hutch facilitates cleaning. Alternatively, a pull-out droppings board can be used.

Mesh attached to outside of wall

Weldmesh panel set in floor

Concrete floors are essential for a floor system, for rats are highly intelligent and devious in their efforts to gain entrance into an area where there are vulnerable young birds. Wood shavings or sawdust provide the best litter material. They are clean, absorbent and also absorb smells, but do ensure that they have been produced for bird use, in case there are toxic residues from the timber.

Suspended feeders and drinkers are probably best in this sort of situation, for they are less likely to have litter scratched into them.

A less intensive floor system for those who like to give their birds more freedom, is one which has the inside run extending outside. An example is shown in the illustration on page 41. Here, the birds range on the concrete floor with wood shavings inside the house. They can also range on a concrete run outside because the run is rat-proof. Outside droppings can be swept with a broom, and if necessary, hosed down when the birds are confined inside by closing the pop-hole. Naturally, woodshavings are not used in the outside run, but it may be a good idea to provide a shallow, dustbath area of fine sand so that they can take dustbaths in fine weather.

Chinese Painted Quail

Male Asian Blue (Chinese Painted).

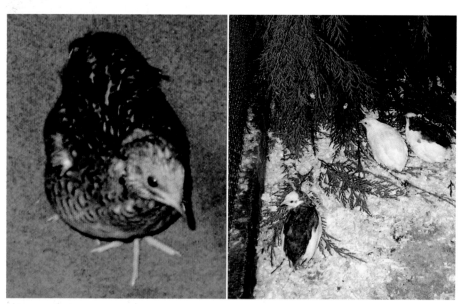

Female Pearl Chinese Painted.
(Quails from Wales)

Pied and White Chinese Painted.
(Quails from Wales)

A group of mixed colour Chinese Painted quail. (*Quails from Wales).*

Male Asian Blue Chinese Painted.

Female Silver Chinese Painted.

Chinese Painted in a grass ranging ark with a Fawn Laying Coturnix on the right..

Comparison of egg sizes from left to right: Chicken, Coturnix, Chinese Painted.

Two ways of using a floor system for quail

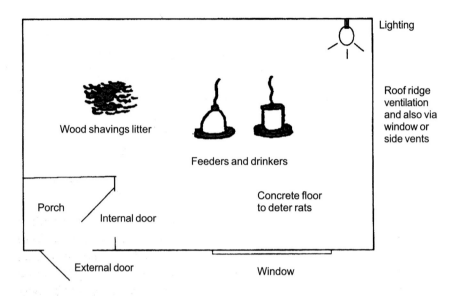

Lighting

Roof ridge ventilation and also via window or side vents

Wood shavings litter

Feeders and drinkers

Concrete floor to deter rats

Porch

Internal door

External door

Window

Here, an open house system is used, where all the birds are in the same area. The porch with the external and internal doors prevents any escapes and also provides draught protection. Artificial light to provide a maximum of 15-16 hours of light encourages egg production.

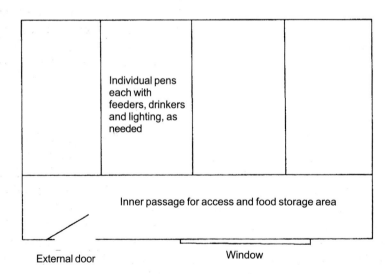

Individual pens each with feeders, drinkers and lighting, as needed

Inner passage for access and food storage area

External door

Window

Here, the area is divided into several pens with access from an internal passage which acts as a porch and a food storage area.

Less intensive system with acess to an outside run via a pop-hole

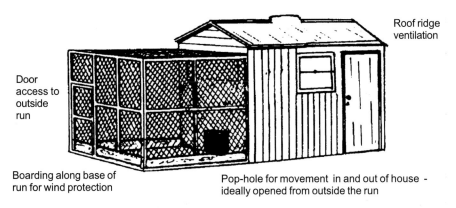

Roof ridge ventilation

Door access to outside run

Boarding along base of run for wind protection

Pop-hole for movement in and out of house - ideally opened from outside the run

The outside run is enclosed by stout wire mesh of a gauge too fine to allow rodents to enter and the bottom section has protective boards which help to protect against the wind. It is at least 90cm (3ft) high with a gate for human access, making run clearance easier. (Perching quail would benefit from a higher run). The provision of a certain amount of natural cover will be welcomed by the birds. Some conifer branches placed in one corner are suitable, or conifer trees in pots. Bracken cuttings and various logs have also been used to good effect. Even if the run is completely contained within a building, the provision of such cover is appreciated.

The great disadvantage of floor systems from the viewpoint of the commercial egg producer, is that quails will not use nest boxes, and will lay their eggs anywhere. This does mean that they are more prone to damage and dirt. Many egg producers raise the young on floor systems then transfer them to cages when they begin to lay.

Aviary systems

Quail breeders and keepers of ornamental or rarer species of quail often use an aviary system, particularly because of the need of some species to perch. The simplest aviary is a small house with attached run, or a bank of these arranged in such a way that the individual runs are parallel with each other, but separate, so that different breeds are kept apart. It is normal for specific breeds to be kept in pairs or trios, but several pairs should not normally be kept together because the males may fight. Most hen birds of the same variety can usually be housed together, although there are always exceptions.

There are many purpose-built aviaries available from specialist suppliers, and they can be most attractive, particularly in a garden setting. Many of them are designed for both flying birds and ground orientated ones.

Other Breeds of Quail

The author's male Common Bobwhite.

Male Cinnamon Bobwhite. (*Quails from Wales*).

Bobwhite male on the right seen sharing an aviary with a British Range Coturnix.

Blue Scaled quail. *(Quails from Wales)*

Californian quail. *(Quails from Wales)*

Mountain quail. *(Quails from Wales)*

Rain quail. *(Quails from Wales)*

Male Mearns quail. *(Quails from Wales).*

Male Harlequin quail. *(Quails from Wales).*

A Permanent Aviary Run

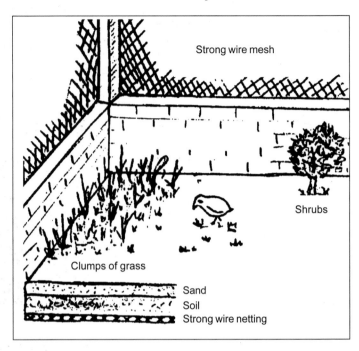

Strong wire mesh

Brick wall or boarding to provide wind protection.

Shrubs

Clumps of grass

Sand
Soil
Strong wire netting

Small aviary built onto a conservatory

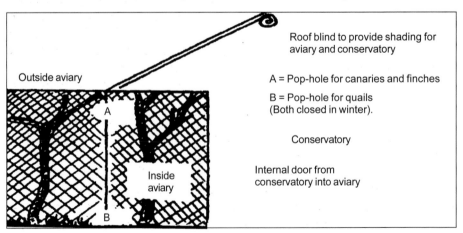

Outside aviary

A

Inside aviary

B

Roof blind to provide shading for aviary and conservatory

A = Pop-hole for canaries and finches

B = Pop-hole for quails
(Both closed in winter).

Conservatory

Internal door from conservatory into aviary

This combined aviary/conservatory allows winter and summer accommodation

A range of aviaries suitable for quail and finches.

Breeders of the more ornamental varieties like to have runs with natural vegetation. It is possible to arrange this, as long as precautions to deter rats are taken. I have already referred to the fact that concrete runs are the safest, but strong wire mesh laid on the ground and extending beyond the perimeter is a good alternative. Once in position, rubble is placed on top, followed by soil and a layer of sand. Small shrubs or other plants can then be planted directly into the soil. Long grasses are particularly suitable for they emulate the conditions which quail frequent in the wild.

As long as there is a quiet, protected corner with such plants, many quail breeds will build nests and incubate their eggs. The Chinese Painted quail, for example, will make a nest in the middle of a clump of long grass. It is said that Coturnix breeds will not become broody, but I have known them to be so, particularly in their second year.

It is necessary to sound a note of warning about the type of netting used underneath the soil in runs such as this. I once used netting which was slightly rusty. I reasoned that it was not good enough for anything else but was quite suitable for putting under the soil. It was a grave error! Rats discovered a weak point and burrowed under the perimeter wall, coming straight up in the centre of the run. They killed the three Japanese quail, one male and two females, which were residents.

Good healthy birds are required for breeding. These are the author's Japanese quail.

When the male deposits foam balls on the ground it is an indication that breeding is imminent. The pound coin indicates the relative size.

A range of eggs ready for incubation. *(Quails from Wales).*

Coturnix quail eggs showing the variation in shell markings.

Egg cartons to fit quail eggs are available.

46

Newly hatched quail. *(Brinsea Incubators).* Japanese Tuxedo chick. *(Quails from Wales).*

Normal Coturnix layer chick. Mexican Speckled Bobwhite. *(Quails from Wales)*

Right:
Pied Bobwhite
chicks.
*(Quails from
Wales).*

47

Design for a Small House and Run that can be moved

Roof overhangs part of run to give added rain and wind protection   Open-air mesh roof

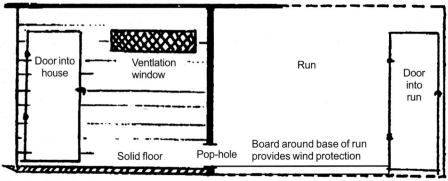

Door into house

Ventilation window

Run

Door into run

Solid floor   Pop-hole   Board around base of run provides wind protection

Wooden skids allowing unit to be moved to a new site

Wire mesh base to run allows access to grass but prevents entry of predators

A really rat-proof floor can be provided by using flag stones instead of netting. These placed close together will exclude even the most devious of rats, while the cracks between them will provide necessary drainage. Soil and finally sand can then be placed on top as before. Sand is recommended because it does allow the birds to make their own dustbathing depressions, as well as providing a popular scratching area. Some breeders also recommend this as a means of deterring earthworms from coming to the surface. Earthworms are hosts to a number of parasites.

An outside aviary run also needs protective walls at the base, with wire mesh above. This can be brick, block or wood, and provides wind protection. Within such an aviary any stout house which is rain and draught-proof is suitable. In milder areas of the country, hardier breeds can be left in outdoor runs as long as the house is well insulated.

Chinese Painted quail are frequently kept in aviaries where tree perching birds are kept because they help to clear up the seeds dropped by the flying birds. This should not be regarded as the sole source of food for them however. It is not enough, for they need a properly balanced diet like any other species. (See the section on *Feeding*). In this context, I should mention a lady who kept Java finches as her prime interest. She had put several Chinese Painted quail into the bottom of the aviary because someone had told her they were useful to clean up aviary floors. She telephoned me to say that they *"kept dying"* and did I know why? During the course of the conversation it emerged that not only did they have no food other than what the finches dropped, but had no house or any form of shelter other than the

One of the author's home-made grazing arks with a range of different quail on the grass.

sapling which was planted in the aviary. Yet the Java finches had a proper diet and sheltered accommodation. No wonder the poor little Painteds died!

Chinese Painted quail are ground-orientated birds and need to have proper rations and clean water provided for them in suitable containers on the ground, rather than having to rely on the occasional spilt seeds falling like manna from above. They also need proper housing which will provide warmth and shelter, free of damp and draughts. A simple house is all that is necessary, but it needs wood shavings or other warm nesting material to provide insulation.

The moveable house and run

If small numbers of Coturnix or Chinese Painted quails are to be kept outside an aviary or house, the best solution is to use a strong house and run of the type used by poultry keepers for hens and chicks. (Bobwhite and larger breeds should be in an aviary).

A small house and run can be moved from one area of grass to another, allowing access to clean pasture on a regular basis. The house needs a well boarded floor capable of deterring rats, so that once shut up for the night the birds are safe from harm. The run which has a wire floor resting on the grass, is obviously safer than the floorless type.

With such a system, it is a good idea to keep specific breeds together, rather than mix them up, although females of the various Coturnix varieties will cohabit successfully. Males housed together may fight and should, as a rule, be kept separate from each other. One male can usually accompany up to around half a dozen females, although with rarer breeds, a ratio of 1:2 or 3 may be preferable. It is worth remembering that Chinese Painted quail are monogamous, and in a colony situation will form pairs.

While a small house and run may be satisfactory in the warmer months, it may not necessarily be successful in winter. My own practice was to have the birds in a house and run in summer and then to transfer them to indoor breeding hutches for the winter. It is possible, in milder areas of the country to have quails in outdoor houses and runs in winter, but precautions must be taken to protect them in more severe winters. However, I have heard of a lady in the South of England who has a few quail completely free-ranging in her back garden all year. I hope they have a warm house at night!

Three types of drinker. The galvanised one on the left can be suspended if necessary. The plastic one in the middle is free-standing while the one on the right clips onto a cage or hutch front.

Feeding

So the old woman began to feed the bird with twice as much food as she had
given it before; but ere long it grew so fat and sleek
that it left off laying any eggs at all.

(Aesop's Fables)

Quails need a relatively high protein ration - around 24% when they are growing, reducing to around 20% once they are fully grown, but there are variations depending on the type of quail. Those that are scheduled as layers need a higher concentration of calcium and phosphorus to cater for the egg shells, while table birds need proportionally less of these.

Quail feeds

The diet needs to include protein, fats, carbohydrates, vitamins and minerals to cater for growth, energy, metabolism and the maintenance of good health. All these constituents are found in proprietary feeds which are formulated to provide a balanced ration.

Proteins, fats, carbohydrates and oils are all found in soya, maize and other cereals. These also provide fibre, a necessary constituent for effective nutrition to take place. A certain level of vitamins and minerals are present in plant proteins, but if there is insufficient, they are added as supplements within a proprietary ration. Different amino acids such as methionine and lysine are also found in plant proteins, and are vital for healthy growth. Methionine also contains sulphur which is needed for good feathering.

At one time, there were no proprietary feeds available for quail and those who kept them either had to buy a game feed or one formulated for turkeys. Now, specific feeds are available, either as proprietary quail pellets or as a quail mix of different small grains. Larger quail such as Bobwhites can be fed on a normal mixed grain ration.

Proprietary chick crumbs are often fed for the first six weeks. These normally contain a coccidiostat to protect against coccidiosis, but coccidiostat-free crumbs are also available from suppliers.

Once the birds have reached their productive stage, at around six weeks old, they need an adult ration. Quail layers' pellets are formulated to meet all the nutritional requirements of laying quail, but without the inclusion of medications. Typical ingredients are: maize, wheat, soya, minerals, fat, limestone grit, vitamins, minerals and methionine. The composition of quail pellets includes 5% oil, 20% protein, 2.7% fibre and 11% ash (mineral content). Pellets are manufactured to a size of 2.5mm so they are suitable for quail.

Nutritional Requirements of Coturnix Quail				
Age/Type	Protein	Methionine	Calcium	Phosphorus
Layer: 0-6 weeks	24%	0.50%	0.85%	0.60%
Table: 0-6 weeks	24%	0.50%	0.85%	0.60%
Layer from 6 weeks	20%	0.45%	2.75%	0.65%
Table from 6 weeks	18%	0.40%	0.65%	0.50%

Based on a number of sources, including Mississipi State University & Florida State University,

An adult Coturnix quail will consume an average of 130g of proprietary pellets a week. Larger quail will obviously eat more. Temperature fluctuations will also have a bearing on consumption for all birds eat more in winter in order to keep warm.

A quail mix of various grains is more difficult to estimate in terms of consumption for the type and ratio of grains will vary, but twice a day feeding where the feed is consumed in about fifteen minutes is reasonable.

Bear in mind that when it comes to feeding, too much can be just as harmful as too little. An obese bird will be less productive and in the long term, liable to health problems. With my rule-of-thumb approach, I find that one of my handfuls (I have small hands) is enough for six Coturnix quail at a time, and I feed morning and afternoon. This is fairly general, of course, and there are bound to be variations.

Home-formulated ration

It is also possible to make up your own feed, of course, and a suggestion is as follows:

1 part oatmeal: 1 part chick crumbs: 1 part millet: 1 part shelled canary seed.

Alternatively, 1 part chick crumbs: 1 part canary seed: 1 part millet.

Bear in mind the need to use only chick crumbs without a coccidiostat if you are making up a ration in this way. It would obviously not be a good idea to be utilising ingredients with an antibiotic additive on a regular basis, as this can lead to antibiotic tolerance and the encouragement of new, stronger strains of pathogens.

It is worth mentioning that for the newly-hatched chicks of Chinese Painted quail even chick crumbs may prove to be too coarse for the first few days. They can be ground up quite easily.

Two types of feeder suitable for quail. The one on the left has inserts to prevent the food being scratched out. The one on the right is designed to clip onto a cage or hutch front. It can also be used as a drinker as shown in the photograph on page 50.

Feed equipment

Quail are inveterate scratchers and will propel their food in all directions if given the opportunity to do so. Those in commercial cage systems will probably have external feed troughs so that only the head can reach them. (See the photo on page 32). Where a floor system is used, suspended feeders which are clear of the ground are the most suitable. If they are gravity-fed or hopper type feeders, the surface area presented to the bird is small enough to prevent jumping up and scratching, yet gravity fills up the feeding area as the feed is eaten. I have found that using flat open containers is a waste of time. The quail merely jump in and scratch the food everywhere. However, there are small feeders available with cross bars which help to keep the food in one place. There are also ones that clip onto a cage or hutch front. (See the photo above). A feed bin for storage is essential. Any dampness in the feed will quickly produce moulds which in turn, lead to mycotoxins that are fatal to the birds. Feed bins and scoops are available from suppliers. Alternatively, a household bin with a tight-fitting lid is suitable.

Water

Clean water is essential at all times and there is no question of just making this available a couple of times a day. It must be there whenever the birds feel like drinking, which could be anytime. Again, a commercial unit will normally have an automatic system which utilises a header tank, tubing, connectors and the drinkers themselves. In a floor system, suspended drinkers as part of an automatic system work well. On a smaller scale, suspended drinkers which operate on a gravity-principle are satisfactory. This is the type I always used for my quail, and they only needed refilling once a day to ensure a supply of water for 24 hours. When my quails were brought inside to their wooden breeding cages for the winter, I used parrot drinkers which clip onto the bars at the front.

Grit

If grains such as millet or chopped wheat are given, then grit is essential otherwise the gizzard which is responsible for grinding up the grain particles cannot function properly. On a commercial scale, where feed may be made available on a conveyor system, the grit can be incorporated into the feed at the mixing stage. On a smaller scale, the odd handful given separately on the ground, or in a small container from which they can help themselves is sufficient. Fine grit suitable for quail is available from most pet shops or aviary suppliers. Grit supplied for chickens may prove to be too coarse for quail. Branded supplies often contain added minerals which help to keep the stock healthy. If cuttlefish is provided for beak care, this can also provide roughage and calcium for the digestive system.

Green food

Quail quickly shred garden greens with their sharp beaks, and it is arguable that this activity has a beneficial effect in preventing feather pecking or other aggressive behaviour, rather than the strictly nutritional benefits. Most commercial quail would not have access to green food, although it is my belief that quail are healthier, happier and longer-lived when they have a good basic diet with lots of variety. Make sure the plants are clean before hanging them up for the birds to peck at. They will soon shred them. It is important not to give too much at a time in case of digestive upsets. For the same reason, it is important to clear away any left over pieces. Giving a little green food about twice a week is enough. Obviously, any weeds should come from your own garden, rather than where they may have been subjected to pesticide sprays, dogs or vehicle exhaust fumes.You don't have any weeds in your garden? It's not like mine, then!

Sprouted grains: including sunflower seeds and those in finch mixtures.
Garden greens: Lettuce. Parsley (Curled and Hamburgh types). Spinach.Chicory.
Garden weeds: Chickweed, *Stellaria media.* Fathen, *Chenopodium album*
Groundsel, *Senecio vulgaris.* Dandelion, *Taxacum officinale*

Breeding

Why should one quarrel with good breeding?
(Eugene Onegin, 1833)

Breeding is an essential aspect of keeping quail, whether on a large or a small scale. It is possible to breed your own replacement birds or buy them in from a specialist breeder.

Smaller enterprises, which often have the coloured and ornamental breeds, generally find that breeding such stock has a ready market among interested poultry keepers, rare breed enthusiasts and aviary owners. Whatever the scale, breeding quail has a fascination which few could doubt. I find it the most interesting aspect of all. The key factor is to obtain good breeding stock to start with, and it is here that a specialist supplier can help. They are listed at the end of the book.

Breeding stock

It goes without saying that the breeding stock should be healthy, have no visible defects and ideally be unrelated. The latter consideration is often overlooked, and purchasers of a pair of a particular breed, may unknowingly have acquired a brother and sister.

Such inbreeding can result in genetic defects being thrown up in the progeny. I once found that a clutch of Japanese Coturnix chicks had three born without claws on the feet. They were the progeny of a pair which I had bought specifically as breeders, although to be fair to the supplier, I did not stress this at the time of purchase. If I had, perhaps the story might have been different. What I should have done, of course, was either to have ensured that they were from different lines, or to have acquired them from different sources. I could also have bought two pairs, one from each source, and swapped over the males.

The use of leg rings is essential in order to keep adequate records and to ensure that you know which bird is which. Normal poultry leg rings are too large, but quail rings are available from specialist suppliers. They can be obtained in different colours, and in a numbered sequence if required. They are available in plastic or aluminium.

Before collecting eggs for incubation, the male and females should have been confined together in breeding quarters for at least a week, and it is as well to discard the eggs for incubating for the first few days afterwards (although they should still be collected) until they have settled down into a

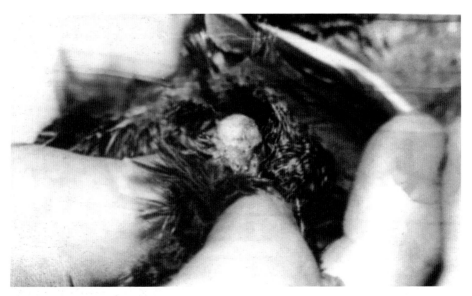

The production of foam balls by the male is a sure sign that he is sexually active. *(Mark Bomer)*

regular output. It is worth mentioning that where different breeds have been kept together, the breeding hens should be separated for two to three weeks before being introduced to the chosen breeding male. This will ensure that there is no possibility of cross-bred fertile eggs being produced.

It is important to ensure that breeding birds are adequately fed. Normal feeds may not supply enough of certain minerals, and a deficiency in the parents can lead to deficiency diseases in the chicks. Special mineral and vitamin pre-mixes are available for adding to the normal ration.

Breeding ratio

Coturnix quail can be kept in pairs, trios or one male for 5 - 6 females where they are kept in a colony. It is worth remembering that hens can be damaged by too much attention from the male, so having more than one with the male can be advantageous. Bobwhites are normally kept in pairs, although there is no reason why the number of females should not be increased. Chinese Painted quail are naturally monogamous and should be kept in pairs, although in a colony, they will pair off. The rarer, ornamental breeds are usually kept in pairs or trios. If you want to keep a precise record of which hen is producing which egg, then the obvious solution is to house only a pair in the breeding quarters for a period of time. Selective breeding for a particular characteristic is made much easier in this way.

Selective breeding may be for a number of reasons: colour, feather markings, egg production, quick growth, weight - and so on. The basic principle

Female Coturnix hen showing where the head feathers have been pulled by the mating actions of the male. Feathers on the sides and back may also be affected.

which operates is that if you breed from two birds which both have a similar characteristic, their progeny will tend to have the same feature, although it is not quite as simple as this for some genetic factors may be dominant, while others are recessive. (See page 73).

In many commercial Coturnix units, it is normal to have one male to each four hens in the cages and mixed running is no problem as far as commercial egg sales are concerned. The eggs are collected every morning and graded. The large and the small ones are usually selected for selling, while the medium-sized ones are often retained for incubation. Of those hatched, many will be reared as table birds, while some are retained as future breeders. Stock birds which are eventually selected from these are then housed in trios in separate breeding accommodation.

The onset of lay

Coturnix quail will start to lay at around 5-6 weeks old, and the eggs will be fertile from about 6-7 weeks onwards. The behaviour of the male will leave no doubt as to when the fertile stage is reached because he will produce 'foam balls' and deposit them on the ground. Once sexually active, he will mate frequently with the females, gripping the feathers on the top of their heads with his beak. There may be head feather loss as a result. (See above).

Quail Incubation Chart

Breed	Day 1 to Pipping	Hatching	
Coturnix varieties	15 days	18 days	**Egg storage before**
Chinese Painted	12 days	16 days	**incubation**
Bobwhite	20 days	23 days	Temperature:
Californian	19 days	22 days	Up to 7 days: 15°C. More than 7 days: 12°C.
Scaled	20 days	23 days	Humidity: 75%
Mearns	21 days	24 days	**Incubation Room**
Mountain	21 days	24 days	Temperature: 20° - 25°C Humidity: 75%
Gambel's	19 days	22 days	

Incubator Temperatures

Allow eggs to come up to room temperature before putting in incubator.

Day 1 to Pipping: 37.5°C. Pipping to Hatch: 37.0°C

Relative Humidity

Day 1 to Pipping: 45%. Pipping to Hatch: 75%

To Convert Celsius to Fahrenheit

Multiply by 9; divide by 5; add 32

Percentage Weight Loss

Quail eggs need to lose 11-13% of their weight during incubation. This formula can be used to calculate it from the weight of one trayful:

$$\% \text{ weight loss at (Day 10)} = \frac{\text{Day 0 egg weight - Day 10 egg weight}}{\text{Day 0 egg weight}} \times 100$$

$$\text{Average daily loss} = \frac{\% \text{ weight loss (Day 10)}}{10}$$

Projected loss at 15 days (Coturnix pipping) = Average daily loss X 15

To Calculate Fertility Percentage

Number of fertile eggs = a   Number of eggs fertile at candling = b

$$\text{Percentage of fertile eggs} = \frac{b \times 100}{a}$$

To Calculate Hatch Percentage

Number of fertile eggs = b   Number of eggs hatched = c

$$\text{Percentage of fertile eggs hatched} = \frac{c \times 100}{b}$$

Occasionally the skin is pierced leaving a wound. If this happens, the female should be removed immediately, in case the bloodstain incites aggressive attack. A period in a hospital cage in solitary confinement will soon enable her to recover.

Occasionally, a male will object to a particular female for no apparent reason, attacking her in a vicious way. When this happens, there is no other solution but to split them up permanently. I have tried to 'improve on nature' in this respect, by keeping them together, but nature obviously knows more than I do, because it always ends in failure.

Storing eggs prior to incubation

Only the best, undamaged eggs from unrelated breeders should be selected for incubation. Once selected, they should be incubated as soon as possible, and ideally no later than a week after being laid. Some will incubate successfully after this, but hatchability begins to decline after a week. (If you have no choice but to keep them longer, reduce the storage temperature to 12°C). Normally, eggs need to be stored, blunt end up, in a cool room at 15°C with a relative humidity of 75%.

The eggs are turned regularly through 45° until they are put in the incubator. On a small scale they can be placed in clean egg cartons or trays, with one end balanced on a support, while a second support stops it slipping. The carton is then tipped in the other direction, with the change taking place at least daily. Plastic insert trays from incubators also make ideal storage holders, and are easily washed and sterilised before use. In this sense, they are preferable to cardboard egg cartons or trays.

Egg cleaning

One of the major causes of poor hatches is the presence of pathogens which cause disease. Eggs should be collected frequently and with clean hands; thin surgical gloves are favoured by many breeders. If the eggs are slightly dirty they can be brushed clean with a dry nailbrush, but beware of damaging the shell!

Dipping the eggs in water to which an egg sanitant has been added is an effective way of minimising disease. Incubator suppliers usually sell sanitants under a number of different brand names. Follow the instructions for a particular brand for their relative strengths can vary. A crucial factor is ensuring that the water is *hand warm* so that any bacteria on the shell surface are drawn away from the pores. If the water is colder than the egg, the effect can be to draw *in* the bacteria! Leave the eggs to drain and dry before placing in the incubator.

The Essentials of Incubation and Hatching

Temperature: 37.5 °C at centre of egg, reducing to 37°C for hatching.
Humidity: 45% increasing to 75% for hatching.

Good, healthy and ideally unrelated breeding stock with proven performance.

Store fertile eggs at 15°C at a relative humidty of 75%, with blunt end up, and at angle of 45°. Reverse direction of tilt twice daily. Incubate before 7 days old.

Ideally use a modern incubator with automatic controls

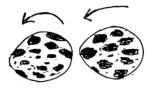

Dip eggs in an egg sanitant and incubate at 37.5°C. Reduce temperature to 37°C three days before hatching.

During incubation, the relative humidity is 45%, increasing to 75% two days before hatching.

If the incubator does not have an automatic turning facility, turn the eggs 3-5 times a day. Wash your hands before handling them.

Candle after 6-7 days, if you must, to see which eggs are developing and discard 'clears'. May not be worth it if incubation time is a short one. NB. Some patterned eggs are difficult to candle.

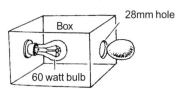

28mm hole

Box

60 watt bulb

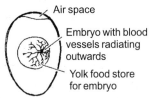

Air space

Embryo with blood vessels radiating outwards

Yolk food store for embryo

After hatching, wait until the chicks are dry and fluffed up before moving them to a protected brooding area with heat lamp, food and water.

For details of incubation times and variations for specific breeds see Page 58.

Natural incubation

Coturnix quail are not particularly good mothers in captivity, although they may become broody and sit on their own eggs if conditions are acceptable. They are more likely to do this in an aviary where a certain amount of natural cover and vegetation is present. They can cover about ten eggs at a time. Most Coturnix eggs are incubated artificially but small broody hens such as Silkies or Pekins have been used successfully, although I have never tried it. In the first issue of this book I asked whether any readers had succeeded in hatching quail by natural methods, and received the following letters:

Coturnix quail

One of my Pekin bantams raised 6 quails without any trouble. She sat on 7 eggs and treated them as her own chicks. I kept them in a small pen with very small wire, and used a drinker of the free-standing type which is used for small cage birds. For the feeder I had the base of a drinker which usually holds an upside-down bottle. Although this is only a one-off experiment, I can't see why it shouldn't work well with any calm type of bantam. I took the mother away at 3 weeks and moved the quails to an aviary at 4 weeks. (Elaine Samson. St. Andrews, Australia)

Chinese painted quail

One year, a pair of Chinese Painted quails earmarked a sandy corner of the aviary as their own. It was quite by accident that I came across the little nest behind some logs under a shrub. The female was sitting there, motionless, while the male paraded up and down indignantly, doing his best to shoo me away. I crept away and left them to it, disturbing them as little as possible, other than providing food and water nearby. I was also worried about the finches flying above, so I erected some netting around the little family's area. To my delight, she hatched four little ones, although one died within a few days. I kept a careful eye on the male in case he attacked them but he was as good as gold. I did make sure that the finches were kept clear until the chicks were several weeks old, just in case, but I don't know whether I was being too cautious. (Jane Hamilton, Surrey, England)

Bobwhite quail

I don't keep quail, although my grandson has some Pharoahs, but I thought you'd welcome hearing about the Bobwhites that took up in my woodlot. I'd heard their whistles for a while before I found the nest. It was just inside the tree-line, in a little hollow, with the cutest grass roof you could imagine.

I kept away as much as possible, and only saw the sitter for a short while. The little brood hatched when I wasn't looking, too, but I guess they survived - at least until the hunters got them. From the egg shell remains there seem to have been around five chicks. I left some chicken feed and water nearby for them so maybe I gave them a good start. (E. Hurst, Mississipi, USA)

Bantam hens can be used to incubate, hatch and brood quail. This is a Partridge Pekin so the feathered legs are clipped in case the quail chicks become entangled in them.

It is more usual to incubate the eggs artificially. Here Coturnix eggs are being set in trays prior to incubation. *(Poultry World)*.

Artificial incubation

Most quails are incubated artificially and certainly on a commercial scale it is essential. Large units will have a separate setting room and incubation room, or at least a separate setter and hatcher. The first caters for the eggs until they are at the initial 'pipping' or cracking stage. The latter is where the trays of eggs are moved for the actual hatching. On a small scale, the incubator will either have separate shelves for setting and hatching, or at least, a hatching tray in the setting area. On a small scale, most general purpose small incubators are satisfactory for quail. I have used several types of incubator over the years and have usually had reasonable results for quail, poultry and waterfowl with them. It must be said, however, that the rate of hatchability is generally lower than it is for poultry.

Cleanliness is essential and the incubator should be thoroughly cleaned before use. The eggs should also be cleaned and dipped in an egg sanitant solution, as described earlier.

Essential features of incubation

Whatever scale of incubation is practised, the salient factors are the same:

Position of incubator The incubator needs to be placed in a room which is at normal room temperature (the equivalent of a spare bedroom). If it is put in an outside shed, the humidity is generally far too high and dead embryos are the result, a condition usually referred to as 'dead in shell'.

Insulation The incubator needs to be properly insulated to minimise heat loss, without restricting ventilation.

Ventilation An adequate flow of air to provide oxygen for the developing embryos and to disperse carbon dioxide is essential. A still-air incubator relies on the opening and closing of air vents, while a fan-assisted one has a built-in fan to do the job. The latter is certainly a feature worth having if you are thinking of buying a new incubator.

Turning Regular turning is essential, if the developing embryo is not to stick to one side of the shell membranes, with a resulting malformation of the embryo. A quail breeder in the West Country, told me that he had consistently poor hatchings with a manually operated incubator, and when he went over to using an incubator with automatic turning facilities, his problems ceased. If manual turning is necessary, the eggs will need to be turned at least 3 times a day, and ideally 5 times. Place a cross on one side of each egg so that you know which side ought to be facing upwards for each particular turn. The markings on Coturnix eggs can make this difficult, so using a bright colour is a good idea.

A small table-top and fan-assisted incubator with automatic roller turning facility and thermostatic controls. The drawer at the front is for water. The egg tray at the back is for hatching.

Temperature During the incubation period, the optimum temperature is 37.5°C at the centre of the egg. In a still-air incubator, where there tend to be fluctuations in temperature in different parts of the container, it may need to register as 39.5°C when the thermometer is held 5cm above the eggs, so that 37.5°C is the reading in the centre of the egg. The advice given by the incubator manufacturer is crucial in this respect.

Remember to run the incubator for 24 hours before introducing the eggs, and also allow the eggs to come up to room temperature before putting them in. The former action will indicate any potential problems with the machine, while the latter avoids a 'shock' to the fertile eggs.

A few days before hatching, the eggs will 'pip'. This is the initial stage when the little birds position themselves to break through the shell. At this stage, the temperature is reduced slightly to 37.0°C to allow for the fact that the birds are themselves generating heat. Turning of the eggs also ceases at this stage.

Humidity The relative humidity indicates the amount of moisture in the atmosphere. During the setting period it needs to be at 45% inside the incubator. This ensures that enough moisture can be lost from the egg, allowing the air space to grow sufficiently for the embryo to breathe. From day one to pipping, quail eggs need to lose 11-13% of their water content. If humidity is too high, it results in the 'dead-in-shell' phenomenon. If too low, the bird will be unable to break out of the shell. At the pipping stage, the relative humidity in the incubator or hatcher is increased to 75% to compensate for this. This is normally achieved by adding extra water, but follow the instructions for your own incubator.

Relative humidity can be measured with a hygrometer. Many small incubators are now equipped with these or you can buy one at most DIY stores. They allow the relative humidity to be measured, but do not control it. If it is necessary to reduce humidity, it is a matter of not adding water to the water tray. Small dehumidifiers which work in conjunction with incubators are also available from suppliers. On a small scale it is also possible to use a desiccant such as a heated newspaper put in the base of the incubator.

The most accurate way of determining the amount of water loss is to weigh the eggs. A convenient way of doing this is to weigh a trayful of eggs before they go into the incubator and then re-weigh them a few days later. The formula on page 58 can be used to calculate the average daily loss which in turn, can be used to predict the final weight loss at the time of pipping.

I found that when I moved my incubator from the shed into a spare bedroom which was at normal room temperature, and which had central heating and therefore less humidity, I had noticeably improved hatches. In my book, *Incubation: A Guide to Hatching and Rearing* (3rd edition), there is a comprehensive coverage of the whole process of breeding and incubating, including details of how to make your own incubators and brooders).

Candling
It is possible to candle, or shine a bright light through the eggs, at around 5-7 days, in order to discover which eggs are fertile and developing, and which are not. If they are developing normally the embryo is seen as a red blob with radiating blood vessels against the egg yolk which is its food store. However, I have always found that the speckled nature of quails' eggs makes them difficult to candle effectively, so I stopped doing it. It must also be said that as the incubation period is fairly short, it is hardly worth doing.

Pipping and hatching
As referred to earlier, a few days before hatching, the chicks will get into position for emerging from the shell. This involves cracking the shell from the inside with the beak, a process known as 'pipping'. At this stage, egg turning must obviously cease and the temperature is slightly reduced to cater for the increased warmth from the chicks. At the same time, the humidity is increased to 75% to make emergence easier. If there is insufficient moisture at this stage the cell membranes may become too dry and stick to the chick.

On a large scale, separate incubators and hatchers may be used, with trays of eggs being moved into the hatchers just before the pipping stage. It is best to avoid 'helping' the chicks from the shell, and to leave them until they are fully dried and fluffed up. The remnants of the yolks are still in the chicks' abdomens so feeding is not required until they are moved to the brooding area.

Different types of quail have different incubation times so the salient facts for each are in the table on page 58. Please be aware that the times given are the average and there are always birds that hatch slightly earlier or slightly later. Allow a couple of days either way.

Brooding
The photograph on page 68 shows a brooding area in a building that is secure against rats. Here, the quail chicks are on wood shavings with heat provided by overhead brooding lamps. It should be mentioned that when the chicks first go into the brooder, it is a good idea to place rough sheets of paper or a piece of old blanket on top of the shavings for the first couple of days. This is to provide a foothold for them and to prevent leg splaying problems. Once they are actively walking about, it can be discarded.

Coturnix quail chick in the process of hatching. *(Poultry World)*

Food can be made available in shallow containers or chick feeders which allow the head to enter, but prevent them getting in to scratch out the food. Small, gravity-fed drinkers are also available.

The brooding area is confined to the vicinity of the heat lamps by a temporary wall. In the photograph on page 68 wire netting lined with plastic feed sacks as insulation is being used. Corrugated cardboard arranged in a circle is also effective as an enclosure. Alternatively, plywood sheeting can be used. The space can be made larger as the chicks grow.

As a general rule, heat will be necessary for about three weeks, gradually raising the lamps to harden off the young birds. Initially, the temperature should be 35°C, but this is gradually decreased as shown on page 69. Once the birds are fully feathered, the heat lamp can be dispensed with.

Rather than worrying about checking degrees, an accurate indication of needs is indicated by the behaviour of the chicks. If they huddle in the middle under the lamp, they are cold and the lamp should be lowered. If they are dispersing to the edges, they are too hot, and the lamp should be raised. The outside temperature naturally has an influence, and in particularly cold periods, it may be necessary to extend the period of heating. Similarly, if it is warm the artificial heat can be reduced or withdrawn earlier.

Young Coturnix quail in a protected brooding area. *(Poultry World).*

A dull emitter lamp for brooding young quail. Electrical or gas powered lamps are available.

Brooding Temperatures	
Days	Temperature
1 - 7	35°C (95°F)
6 - 14	32°C (90°F)
15 - 21	29°C (85°F)
22 - 28	27°C (80°F)
29 - 35	24°C (75°F)

From then on reduce as necessary depending on outside temperature.

Height of Lamp

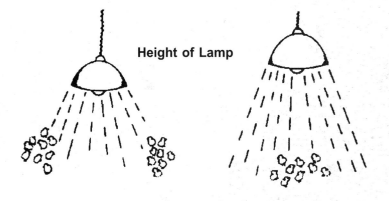

If chicks are ranged around the periphery, they are too hot so raise the lamp.

If chicks cluster in a ball under the lamp they are too cold so lower the lamp.

If they are evenly spaced under the lamp, the height is right.

Problems with young quail

Escaping

Reference has already been made to the fact that young quails are great escapees and that all cracks and crevices in a brooding area must be filled. Also, it may be necessary to put netting over the top.

Drowning

Their tendency to drown easily in shallow water should also be taken seriously, and for the first week, open drinkers need to have clean pebbles or marbles placed in them, so that the depth of water is reduced to a safe level, while still providing water for them to drink.

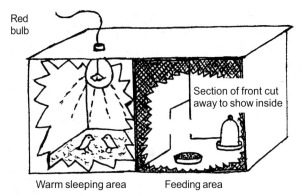

Red bulb

Brooders for a small number of quail chicks

Section of front cut away to show inside

Adapting a rabbit hutch or large cardboard box

Warm sleeping area   Feeding area

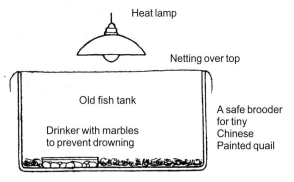

Heat lamp

Netting over top

Old fish tank

Drinker with marbles to prevent drowning

A safe brooder for tiny Chinese Painted quail

An open water container should have pebbles or marbles placed in it to prevent the chicks drowning.

Appropriate food

A starter ration of chick crumbs is suitable for most quail, but for the first few days it may be too big for Chinese Painted chicks. It can easily be crushed to make it appropriate for them.

Chick crumbs are available with or without a coccidiostat to prevent coccidiosis, a digestive disease that can be a killer. As long as chicks are given a clean area without damp litter they are unlikely to get coccidiosis. However, some breeders prefer to let them have the medicated crumbs for the first few weeks and then go over to a coccidiostat-free ration.

Foot and leg problems

A problem with feet which I discovered to my cost some years ago was when I used a brooder with under-floor heating. Although equipped with a thermostat, and having adequate insulation as well as wood shavings litter on top, the whole batch of quail developed the same foot problem. Basically this was a blackening of the toes, followed by rapid withering and ultimately the complete loss of them. The whole batch had to be put down and I have never used this form of brooder again. The problem has never recurred.

Underfloor heating in a brooder can cause foot problems unless it is carefully monitored.

Providing a suitable surface to provide a grip helps to prevent leg splaying. (*Quails from Wales*)

Reference has already been made to the need for flooring with a firm grip for the first few days, until the chicks have found their feet and are active.

Congenital diseases
Where chicks hatch with defects such as crooked body, lack of eye(s), or other obvious defects, it is usually the result of too much in-breeding. The closer the parents are related to each other, the greater the chance of congenital defects in the young.

Deficiency diseases
Parent birds that are inadequately fed have a greater chance of producing defective chicks. The diet may seem to be adequate but if it is formulated for layers rather than breeders, it may be deficient in the right balance of mineral and vitamins. Breeder rations or pre-mix additions are available from specialist suppliers, and these are often the choice of the larger breeder. On a small scale, grass ranging and the ability to forage in the sunshine provide some of the supplements. Wheatgerm provides Vitamin E while yeast, hard-boiled eggs or *Marmite* provide Vitamin B_2. Cod liver oil, or being in the sunshine, provides Vitamin D so that the chicks do not develop Rickets. The following are some of deficiency problems that result from inadequately fed parent birds:

• Clubbed ends to down feathers - Vitamin B_2 deficiency in parents.
• Curly toes - Vitamin B_2 deficiency in parents.
• Splayed legs from Rickets (other than by slipping on unsuitable surfaces in the first few days) - Vitamin D deficiency in parents.
• Head thrown back, gazing upwards - Vitamin E deficiency in parents.

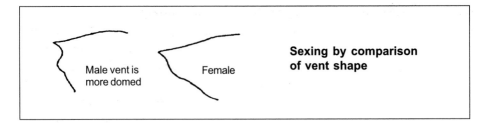

Male vent is more domed

Female

Sexing by comparison of vent shape

Some Hints on Sexing quail

• Normal type Coturnix laying quail are easy to sex because from about three weeks onwards, the reddish brown chest of the male starts to become noticeable. His markings are also more distinct than those of the female.

• Once they are adult and in breeding condition, from about 6 weeks onwards, the sexual behaviour and foam ball production of the male, referred to earlier, will be apparent. Before the age of three weeks, it is virtually impossible to sex the birds, and it is debatable whether it is necessary at this stage anyway.

• Italian Golden hens have a distinctive face mask.

• The coloured varieties of Coturnix, such as English White, Range and Tuxedo do not have an apparent difference in feathering between the male and female, but they can be distinguished by their size difference for the female is bigger than the male.

• As indicated above, the vent of the male is more domed, while that of the female is more inverted. This difference is only seen after they have reached sexual maturity, when their behaviour will indicate their sexes anyway.

• In adulthood, the differences in vocal sounds, mentioned earlier in the book, are also apparent.

• In breeds such as the Bobwhite, Californian, Gambel's, Harlequin and Chinese Painted, the males can be distinguished by their face mask which is absent in the females. However, the White variety of Chinese Painted cannot be distinguished by this feature.

• The Californian male has a distinctive blue-grey breast in addition to the face mask referred to above.

• The Blue Scaled quail is difficult to sex for the male and female have similar crests and plumage, but the female's crest has slightly more buff colour and her chin is slightly striped as compared with the male's plain chin.

• In the Mountain quail, the female's crest is shorter.

Genetics of Colour Mutation in Coturnix Quail

Pigments called melanins determine the plumage colour and markings. Depending on the genetic structure, these pigments are present in various dilutions and ratios. Some of the genes are dominant and will therefore appear more frequently in crossings. Others are recessive and will tend to be masked by the dominant factors, but appearing in small numbers. Others still, are incompletely dominant with the appearance of their factors depending on the particular crosses.

Some crosses are associated with lethal conditions so, if going in for breeding, it is as well to be aware of these and cross with the normal type, rather than with each other. The following are found in Japanese Coturnix quail:

Black at hatch (Bh). This is dominant over other colours but a double dose where two Bh birds are crossed can have lethal consequences with a proportion of eggs failing to hatch.

Cinnamon (Cin). This is a recessive gene producing ginger plumage.

Extended Brown (E). This is incompletely dominant over the normal type. Birds are uniformly brown above and below.

Imperfect albinism (al). This is recessive. Two doses produce albino, pink-eyed and white-feathered chicks.

Redhead (e^{rh}). This is recessive and where it manifests, produces birds that are predominantly white with irregular black and rust plumage. The male's head is rust-coloured.

Silver (B). This is incompletely dominant. It is associated with slow growth and slow sexual maturity when two of the same are crossed.

White breasted (wb). This is a recessive gene. Where it appears it produces birds with a white-feathered breast, neck and face. Both sexes are the same.

Yellow (Y). This is a dominant gene that produces golden birds. If two of the same are crossed, there is a lethal factor that produces fatalities of 25%. Crossing a gold with a brown is safer, producing mainly gold and some brown in the proportion of 2:1.

There are also feather structure mutations associated with Japanese quail:

Defective feathering (Df). This is dominant giving short, sparse feathers.

Porcupine (pc). Recessive producing abnormal furled feathers on the back.

Rough textured (rt). Recessive producing feathers rough to the touch.

Ruffle (rf). Recessive producing soft barbs to some of the feathers.

Short barb (sb). Recessive where ends of the back feathers are short and appear broken. (Ref: Quail Genetics Resource Centre. University of British Columbia).

Eggs

Here's Agamemnon, an honest fellow enough, and one that loves quails.
(Troilus and Cressida. Shakespeare).

Coturnix eggs

Quail eggs are quite rightly regarded as delicatessen items. Their small, speckled appearance is different from the eggs that people are used to buying, and they are associated with quality and the concept of 'something different'. In terms of eating quality, they are equivalent to chicken eggs and have the following nutritional values:

Typical value per 100g - Energy: 682kJ. 164kcal. Protein: 12.8g. Carbohydrate: 1.0g. Fat: 12.1g of which saturates are 7.4g. (*Source:* Fayre Game Egg Pack).

An average Coturnix egg weighs around 10g and the relative size can be seen in the photograph opposite. The size is approximately one fifth that of a chicken's egg. The eggs are off-white splashed with chocolate brown. The latter may be in the form of tiny spots, large spots or large splodges. There is a considerable variation in patterning. I once tried to keep a record of all the variations of patterning, hoping that I would be able to identify particular eggs as belonging to specific hens, without having to trap-nest. I soon gave up because just when I thought I was getting somewhere, a new variation would appear.

They also occasionally produce olive-coloured eggs with no markings at all, just to be perverse. Some strains produce all-white eggs as a mutation. Birds which produce these should obviously not be used for breeding. This whiteness is not to be confused with the bluish white chalky material which is sometimes apparent and which is nothing to worry about.

In the wild, the Coturnix lays about a dozen eggs in a clutch, with several clutches in a season. Japanese quail can produce around 250 eggs while those that have been selectively bred for egg laying are capable of producing over 300 a year under good management and with the provision of supplementary lighting.

In Britain, the same Coturnix quail have, until comparatively recently, been used for egg production as well as for the table trade. In recent years, Jumbo versions of Japanese quail have increasingly been used for the table, while lighter strains such as the Spanish and Italian Golden are kept for eggs. If starting a commercial enterprise, try to buy the best strains available. Once the enterprise is running smoothly, either concentrate on doing your own selective breeding, by maintaining a breeding flock from which

Coturnix eggs can be sold in purpose-made plastic cartons which allow the patterning of the egg to show through for the customer.

future quality birds can be selected, or buy in young replacement stock from specialist breeders. When buying breeders, try and acquire them from different sources so that in-breeding is minimised.

The onset of lay

Laying starts around the age of five to six weeks. Providing supplementary light too early can produce precocious birds that commence laying before their bodily frame has finished growing. Natural light is the best form of lighting and only needs to be supplemented in autumn, winter and spring. Further details are given below.

Most eggs are laid in the afternoon and evening and on average, a hen reaches full production at around 50 days. In the second year, production can fall to nearly half.

Winter eggs

The provision of artificial light in winter is essential if egg production is to continue without disruption. In a small house, a 25 watt bulb is adequate for about a dozen birds and 40 watt for around 50 birds. A 150 watt bulb with a reflector will be sufficient for a 6 x 3m (20′ x 10′) building. Fluorescent tube lighting is also satisfactory. It is essential to incorporate a time-

Packaging should include as much information as possible.

switch in the circuit so that the light is switched on and off automatically. A total of 15-16 hours of light a day (natural plus artificial) will keep egg production at satisfactory levels.

Start giving extra light before dawn or dusk (or a combination of both), gradually increasing the duration to compensate for the shortening days. Similarly, as the days lengthen, gradually decrease the amount of artificial light, as long as the birds are receiving enough natural light. It is important to be consistent in turning on and switching off the light, and it is here that a pre-programmed time-switch is essential.

In winter, the drop in temperature imposes more demands on the metabolism so that a certain proportion of extra energy is needed to keep warm. If necessary, increase the rations accordingly. An important aspect to bear in mind is that giving extra light pre-supposes that the birds are all females. If they have not been separated, the males will fight, and extra light will only aggravate this. If a mixed group of birds are being reared for the table at a relatively early stage, where separation would not be feasible, it is best to restrict light.

Pickled quail eggs are sold as delicacies. Here they are in their shells.

Collecting eggs

Eggs should be collected at least once a day, with cleanliness being observed at all times. This includes washing hands before handling them and putting them in a cool storage area away from any contaminants that might affect them. A cool room is normally between 12°C - 15°C . At present, there is no official system of grading the eggs, as is the case with chickens' eggs.

With a cage system, it is unlikely that there will be any problem of soiling of eggs for they are collected in a rollaway collection area. If there are any lightly soiled eggs it is best to brush them with a clean, dry nailbrush.

Packaging eggs

Packaging is an important aspect of marketing and plastic egg cartons specifically for quail eggs are available from specialist suppliers. If the quantity of cartons purchased is large enough, it is usually possible to have descriptive labels with details of your own farm incorporated. Alternatively, it is possible to order labels that you can stick on yourself. Specialist companies can provide all that is necessary for packaging and labelling requirements.

The photograph opposite shows a carton of quail eggs that I purchased at my local supermarket. The plastic carton, like the one shown on the previous page, has a cardboard sleeve that fits around it, but leaves a space on one side through which the eggs can be seen. There are also pictures of the eggs on the card itself. There is a *Best Before* date on the front of the card, as well as a description of the contents and the names of the producer and distributor. Every space on the cardboard sleeve is used to impart information to the customers. On one side we are told the location of the producer and that the eggs are laid to welfare standards from quail that are fed GM-free feed without growth promoters or routine veterinary products.

On the back of the sleeve nutritional, storage, preparation and serving suggestions are detailed, as well as the name, address, telephone number and website of the distributor.

Traceability requirements are being met, while the customers (who may not have tasted quails' eggs before) are being actively encouraged to try them, and they have plenty of information on how to use them.

Selling eggs

According to DEFRA, the term 'poultry' means chickens, ducks, geese, turkeys and guinea fowl. Quail are not included in the definition. By the same token, quails' eggs do not come under the Egg Marketing Regulations. It makes sense, however, to produce eggs to the same high standard and ensure that they are handled and stored in a hygienic manner.

On a small scale, eggs are best sold in cartons to local customers, but on a large scale, it may be necessary to use the services of a distributor.

Preserved eggs

A common form of egg preservation and marketing is to hard boil the eggs and put them in brine in a glass jar. See the example on the previous page which has six eggs in a jar with a metal crimped-on lid. This particular example is a product imported into the UK from France. Alternatively, cooked, shelled eggs in brine or pickling vinegar are possibilities.

Quail eggs can also be used to produce a prepared product such as miniature Scotch eggs. (Recipes are given later).

Eggs of other breeds

The Coturnix breeds all lay similar looking eggs to the normal laying quail, although there are slight variations. Other breeds are listed below:

Bobwhite

The eggs are slightly bigger than those of Coturnix breeds, and generally have a paler appearance. The background colour is greyish-white and there may be a fine speckling of brown spots. In the wild, up to about two dozen eggs are produced in a season. Selectively-bred specimens in protected conditions can produce 50-100 eggs a year, with no extra light. With the provision of artificial light, the provision of winter quarters and adequate feed rations, this can be increased to 150-200 a year.

Chinese Painted

The eggs are considerably smaller than those of the Coturnix quail. They are brownish-grey colour and there may be some mottling. In the wild, about a dozen eggs are produced in a season. In aviary bred and managed birds, this number can be increased to around 50 or more with the provision of extra light to produce early eggs for incubation.

Californian

Eggs are buff to cream with brown spots. There are usually up to 15 eggs in a clutch, although protected aviary conditions may result in more.

Gambel's

Up to 20 eggs in a clutch is fairly common, and there can be several clutches in a season. Egg shells are pale brown with brown spots.

Mountain

There are up to 15 cream coloured eggs in a clutch.

Blue Scaled

Egg colouring is pale brown with light spots, and there are up to 20 eggs in a clutch, with several clutches a season.

Mearns

Around 6-20 eggs are laid in a clutch, and the shells are white.

Cuttlefish bone enables quail to keep their beaks in trim and also provides minerals.

Quail for the table

I hope we're not having anything difficult this evening, like quails".
(The Mystery of the Blue Train. Agatha Christie)

In Britain, the same strains of Coturnix quail are often used for eggs as well as for the table, although larger Jumbo strains are now available for the table. Some people regard them as a dual-purpose breed for they are quite good layers, although they do not lay as many eggs as the smaller laying strains. In the USA, the Bobwhite is sometimes raised for meat.

A house with a concrete floor is the most appropriate because of the dangers associated with rats which can kill adult quails with ease. Ridge ventilation in association with side windows or vents is ideal, so that ventilation can be controlled. Many producers find that dividing a house into separate pens is better than having one large house. Quails are nervous birds and the tendency to panic and flap in one direction can lead to problems of management. An easy and relatively cheap way of subdividing the floor space is to use game netting, or some other form of lightweight panelling. Most game equipment suppliers sell such products.

Each pen or floor space needs wood shavings or sawdust litter, a suspended or gravity-fed feeder (or one from which the birds cannot scratch food) and ideally, an automatic watering system. Young quail will have artificial heat as described in the breeding section.

Quail meat regulations

In order to sell quails for meat it is necessary to be familiar with the 'meat hygiene' regulations. These vary according to the scale of operations. The regulations governing quails shadow fairly closely those for poultry.

The starting point for information is to contact the *Local Environmental Health Department* who will explain what regulations are applicable in your particular case. The regulations cover the slaughter and sale of fresh or frozen quail meat. Small scale operations, slaughtering less than 10,000 birds a year, are exempt from *Directive 92/116,* but are restricted to selling in their own localities and traditional markets. If you plan a larger operation, producing more than 10,000 but less than 150,000 birds, you still qualify as a 'low throughput plant'. The regulations covering this, and larger scale operations, are available from the *Veterinary Meat Hygiene Advisor.*

Finally, if you plan to export quails or quail meat, there are different regulations contained in the *Animal Health Circular 92/13 7* and the *European Directive on Farmed Game 91/495.* Again, the *Meat Hygiene Advisor* can advise.

Weighing

Some, or indeed all the females, may be separated for future egg production, leaving the males behind for table production. With ordinary Coturnix laying quail the aim will be to produce quail with a liveweight of 160-200g (6-7oz) at the age of 6 weeks, with a conversion ratio of around 3:1. In other words, for every three ounces of food consumed, around one ounce of weight is produced. These days, the Jumbo strain of Coturnix is a better choice for it is claimed that they can achieve a liveweight of 390gm (14oz)

It is not feasible to weigh all the birds, of course, but it is a good idea to take a few sample weighings, using say half a dozen birds. This will give an indication of the average batch weight.

The easiest way to weigh a quail is to use a small bag with a draw string at the top. The bird is popped into the bag, the draw strings tightened and then the whole thing is suspended on a spring balance. It takes only a moment or two, there is no distress caused to the bird, and it is released immediately after weighing.

Ready-made weighing cones and scales, as well as electronic scales, are available from specialist suppliers. Weigh about 6 birds per batch in order to have an average weight every week until killing time.

Keeping records

Everyone has their own system of keeping records. The form is not important. What is necessary is to ensure that all details in relation to weight gain and feed consumed are recorded. Also record costs and any medications.

Table Quail Record Card			
Date hatched: Number:	Average liveweight	Feed consumed	Comments
Week 1 Week 2 Week 3 Week 4 Week 5 Week 6, etc			Losses_____

Light restriction

Table quail grow more quickly and sexual development is slowed down if the amount of light to them is restricted. This does not mean that they have to be kept in a twilight zone, as is the case with so many poultry broilers, but no artificial light should be made available to them, as for egg producers.

Individual quail trussed ready for sale or cooking

Some producers, I am afraid, go to absurd lengths in blocking out the light. I am against this on humanitarian grounds. Every creature has a right to natural light! The aim is to cut down bright light, while allowing a certain amount of natural light to come in. This suppresses the urge to mate and to lay eggs so that growth continues uninterruptedly. In this way, heavier weights are gained. *Marsh Farms* in the USA claim that delaying the onset of lay until 12 weeks of age produces a doubling of normal bodyweight.

Killing, plucking and dressing

There are specialists who offer a slaughtering service, if the scale warrants it. On a small scale, it will probably be the producer himself who carries it out. The usual method of killing is to sever the head in one quick movement. For this, a sharp butcher's knife or cleaver used in conjunction with a wooden block is suitable, although some producers find that sharp shears are effective. Alternatively, poultry equipment suppliers sell a purpose-made poultry killer which operates on a guillotine principle. It is recommended that the publications produced by the Humane Slaughter Association are consulted.

Allow the birds to bleed, but it is not necessary to hang quails as it is with other game birds. Plucking should take place as quickly as possible, and here there are several alternatives:

Dry plucking

This is simply the removal of the feathers without using water or any other medium to assist the process. Plucking by hand can be a rapid process for those experienced in the field, but mechanical dry plucking machines are available where large quantities are involved.

Some people use these for the rough plucking, finishing off the pin feathers by hand, scraping or using a wax finish.

Plucked, gutted and packaged quail ready for sale. *(Poultry World)*

Wet plucking

Here, the bled birds are immersed in scalding water for a moment then removed and plucked as soon as possible. When plucking is complete, they are immersed in chilled water to cool.

Once plucked, the birds are drawn. Traditionally, the innards were not removed and Mrs. Beeton would have frowned on such a practice. Modern susceptibilities however, demand that gutting is as complete as possible and commercial table quails will certainly need to be processed in this way, unless they are being sold by contract to a butcher for processing. Gutting is not as easy as it is with poultry, bearing in mind the relative smallness of the birds. Utilising a spoon inserted in the neck end and rotating it inside the body cavity is effective. Cutting around the vent and enlarging the opening then allows the innards to be drawn out.

Waxing

The principle of waxing is that the birds are dipped in molten wax and as this cools and hardens, the feathers come off with the wax crust. As referred to earlier, some producers use this method as a 'finishing' technique after initial rough plucking.

Some producers find this process too time-consuming, and slit the birds down the back in order to gut them. Some complete the process by boning the birds at the same time, selling the finished product as 'boned quail'. On a large scale, vacuum drawing of the innards is carried out. Once gutted, with the neck cut off close to the body and the legs cut off at the first joint up from the foot, the birds should be chilled again while awaiting packaging. The usual way of packing quail is on polystyrene tray containers and covered with cling film sealed into position. A common procedure is to pack four birds to each tray, arranged neatly, breast-side upwards. The photograph on page 83 shows ten birds packaged in this way, with a label showing the producer's name and the description to say that they are 'English bred quail'.

Oven-ready birds, as described above, can be sold fresh or frozen, depending on the particular market requirements. One great advantage of quail over game birds is that they are available right through the year, rather than on a seasonal basis. This is an important marketing point, in making 'game' dishes available to connoisseurs all through the year.

Smoked quail

A popular delicatessen commodity, smoked quail, is definitely for the top end of the market. If an enterprise is to be expanded in this direction, the best way is to arrange a contract with a local smoking company so that they do it in batches as necessary.

Smoking of food is a skilled task and as there are EU directives with regard to safety, it is better to let a specialist company do it. When selling direct to customers, as for example in a farm shop, being able to give them advice on how to use them is important if they have not had quail before.

Recipes

Just after I wrote the first edition of this book, and my head was still full of quail facts and figures, I went to northern Spain with my husband. On our first evening there we went out for a special meal and I ordered what appeared to be an exotic dish that I had never tried before. When it arrived, it was quail! 'Oh, no!' was my first reaction, but as it happened, the meal turned out to be delicious.

Mrs Beeton's recipe

Ingredients. Quails, butter, toast.
Method: These birds keep good for several days and should be roasted without drawing (*but not if you have modern susceptibilities - author*). Truss them

with the legs close to the body and the feet pressing upon the thighs. Place some slice of toast in the dripping pan, allowing a piece of toast for each bird. Roast for 15-20 minutes; keep them well basted and serve on the toast.

Quick roast quail

Ingredients: Quails, 2 slices of bacon per bird, seasoning
Method: This is my favourite way of cooking them and the bacon adds flavour, as well as preventing too much drying. Wrap up each bird in the bacon and use wooden sausage sticks to keep them in place.

Roast in a medium oven for about 20 minutes and serve with any of the sauces normally used with chicken or game.

Grilled quails

Ingredients: Quails, butter, lemon juice, bacon slices, seasoning, breadcrumbs.
Method: Slit each quail down the backbone. Flatten each side and sprinkle with lemon juice, salt and pepper. Dip in melted butter and roll in breadcrumbs. Grill for about 5-6 minutes on each side.

Meanwhile, roll up the bacon slices and grill them for the last few minutes with the quail. Serve quails with bacon rolls and garnish with mushrooms.

French roast quail

Ingredients: Quails, butter, vine leaves, toast, seasoning, milk.
Method: Wipe quail inside and out. Place in a saucepan with just enough milk to cover them. Simmer gently for 6-7 minutes. Remove and put the saucepan and its contents to one side for the moment. Smear the quail with butter and wrap in vine leaves. Sprinkle with salt and pepper and place in a buttered oven-proof dish. Roast for 10 minutes in a medium oven, then take the dish out of the oven. Strain the contents of the saucepan and pour over the quail. Replace the dish in the oven and cook for another 10 minutes. Serve each quail on a slice of toast and garnish with wedges of lemon and sprigs of parsley.

Miniature Scotch eggs

An enterprising British quail egg producer has evolved a novel way of giving his eggs value-added appeal. He hardboils them, removes the shells, coats them in flour and sausagemeat, with a final coating of breadcrumbs. Once deep-fried for a few moments, they provide miniature Scotch eggs, a delicacy which has obvious appeal for the delicatessen market.

Pickled eggs

Quails' eggs are so attractive that many people hard boil and serve them in their shells. An alternative is to preserve or pickle them in one of the following ways:

Whole eggs in brine

This is a compromise where the eggs are first hard boiled and then placed in a brine solution without removing the shells. A normal brine solution of 50g salt per 600ml of water (2oz per pint) is suitable. Hard boil the eggs, drain and place them in sterilised jars and top up with the brine solution, making sure that they are completely covered. (Jars can be sterilised by washing in hot water, then put upside down on a rack in a warm oven, with the door open).

Home Farm pickled eggs

This is the recipe that I always used for my quails' eggs. Hard boil the eggs, then plunge into cold water to cool and make them easier to peel. (Note that fresh eggs are more difficult to peel than older ones, so don't use really fresh eggs for pickling).

Peel the eggs then place them into sterilised glass jars and top up with a pickling solution made as follows:

Place 1 litre of white wine vinegar or cider vinegar and half a litre of water in a stainless steel pan. (You can leave out or reduce the water if you like a 'tangy' egg, but it does mean that the more delicate egg is dominated by the vinegar). If you have just a few eggs, reduce the ingredient amounts accordingly. Add 2 level tablespoons of salt, a medium sized chopped onion and a sachet of pickling spice, and bring to the boil. Simmer for a few minutes, leave to cool and strain. Pour over the eggs, then pop in some of the boiled peppercorns, just to make the jar look more interesting.

Oak Ridge pickled eggs

This is a recipe from Max and Mary Crawley of Arkansas, USA, and I am grateful to Edmund Hoffman for the information.

Boil the eggs for five minutes in water to which the following have been added: half a cup of salt and 1 fluid oz of vinegar per gallon of water. Cool in cold water and peel the eggs, then place them in sterilised jars.

Prepare the pickling solution as follows: add 1 cup of salt and 1 large chopped onion (with other spices if liked) to two pints of white vinegar and two pints of water. Bring to the boil, drain and pour over the eggs.

Large scale pickled eggs

This recipe is more appropriate to large producers. Hard boil the eggs and then place them in commercial grade, distilled white vinegar for 12 hours. This dissolves the shells, but leaves the membranes intact. Wash the eggs and refrigerate until quite cold then immerse in clean water while the membranes are removed by hand. They are now ready for immersing in the pickling solution of your choice.

Quails' eggs in aspic

Quails' eggs in aspic is, of course, a well-known delicacy and another way of achieving the maximum return on the eggs if they are to be sold. Aspic is available in powder form for mixing as required.

The eggs are hard boiled, then shelled. They can be cracked, placed in cold water and have the shells and membranes removed simultaneously. If cut in half and placed in a small glass or plastic container with the yolk facing upwards, the aspic mixture can then be poured on. Once set and cooled, clear snap-on lids can be placed on the container, enabling the product to be seen. If the container is small containing, for example, four halves, it is a perfect individual hors d'oeuvres.

White Coturnix at rest in the grass.

Health

Healing is a matter of time,
but it is sometimes also a matter of opportunity.
(Hippocrates, c.460-357BC)

Quails, like all living things, require good food, clean water, warm, dry and draught-free housing and regular attention. The main priority is always to prevent trouble and ill health, and to develop a ready eye for problems at an early stage. As soon as anything suspicious is noticed, such as listlessness, poor appetite, discharge from the beak or unusually coloured droppings, it is a good idea to isolate the bird immediately. This does two things; it stops the spread of possible infection to the others, and it allows the invalid a better chance of recovery. Listless birds invite aggression and may be severely pecked by the others.

A hospital cage

A hospital cage is a useful thing to have. This could be a wooden bird breeding cage with a wire front, or even a large cardboard box. Specialist suppliers also sell purpose-made ones. Place some woodshavings in the bottom and clip on a feeder and drinker. The chances are that a sick bird will not be interested in the food, but it will certainly require water.

The cage should be in a warm, sheltered area, but if it is particularly cold, it may be a good idea to have a dull emitter bulb fixed up to provide a source of warmth. This can be placed outside the cage so that it is shining in sideways, through the cage front. Depending on the facilities available, it could be suspended from above. It is surprising how the provision of warmth and cosseting in this way, can sometimes make the difference between survival and loss, when all else possible has been done.

It is obviously not economic to call in the vet to see a single bird, although there is nothing to prevent you taking a container with bird along to the vet. Where the condition is a minor one, such as a cold or simple digestive upset, it will clear up of its own accord, and the protected conditions help to make this sooner rather than later. If it is a more serious condition, there is not a lot to be done, and at least the bird will have met its end in relatively quiet comfort. If the bird is the first casualty in a more general outbreak, it enables action to be taken in time to protect the others.

Commercially, a record of all medicinal treatments should be kept. It makes sense to do so on a small scale, too.

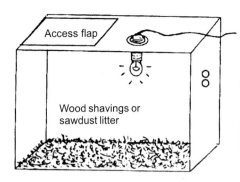

A Home-made Hospital Cage

Access flap

Strong box fitted with dull emitter bulb

Ventilation holes

Wood shavings or sawdust litter

One side can be fitted with mesh to make for easy viewing and also to fit on a feeder and drinker

Bacterial respiratory infections

Illnesses caused by bacteria can be treated with antibiotics, where viral ones can not. Some of the more common bacterial infections which affect the respiratory tract are bronchitis, pneumonia, infectious sinusitis and chronic respiratory disease. They all have similar symptoms of wheezing, laboured breathing, nasal discharge and loss of appetite. Antibiotics are available only from veterinary surgeons. They should be used only when it is advisable to do so, and following the recommended doses. If there is a withdrawal period, where eggs or birds may not be sold or eaten, it is essential to follow the guidelines.

Bacterial digestive infections

Enteritis results in greenish droppings. Coccidiosis produces greenish droppings but of a more slimy nature. Antibiotic treatment is required and the vet will prescribe an appropriate one for dosing the drinking water. Reference has already been made to the fact that some starter rations include a coccidiostat. Salmonella is always a danger, and every effort should be made to avoid it. Make sure that all feeders and drinkers are cleaned regularly and thoroughly, and that feedstuffs are fresh and clean.

Worms

Internal worms may be a problem with quail which are aviary housed, or which have access to the soil via pens. The importance of moving pens to fresh, clean ground on a regular basis is obvious, as well as the practice of liming aviary soil each autumn while the birds are in their winter quarters. Caged quails are unlikely to have worm problems because they are not in a position to ingest the cysts which produce them. Internal worms cause emaciation and loss of feather condition, and any permanent quail breeding stock which has access to the ground, should be wormed as a matter of course before being brought in for the winter. A vermifuge which is licensed for use with gamefowl and poultry is *Flubenvet* which is given in the feed.

Scaly leg

This is a condition of the legs, where burrowing mites push up the scales of the legs and produce white encrustations. It is highly infectious and will spread rapidly to all the birds if not treated quickly. Using a small, soft brush and warm soapy water, soak and very gently brush off the encrustations, then dry the legs before applying a mite killer which is available from the vet or licensed supplier. This is most effective and far better than the traditional paraffin treatment. Do not try and pull the dry encrustations away otherwise the skin itself is pulled away.

Bumblefoot

A hard lump can sometimes form underneath the foot, where a small wound may have healed over leaving some infection behind. It is first detected when a bird is seen to be limping. If the infection is still active, the foot will feel hot and swollen and antibiotic treatment may be needed. If the lump is near the surface, it can be lanced to remove the pus, then treated with a veterinary spray.

Wounds

Wounds such as those acquired by head banging or fighting should be cleaned and treated with a veterinary spray. Keep the bird in isolation until the wound has healed, in case it is pecked by the others.

Mites

Quails can be affected by mites in the same way that poultry beome infested. Red mite is a particular problem. Proprietary insecticide powder or spray is the answer, applied under the wings and around the neck and rump feathers. Several types are available from licensed poultry and pet suppliers. Don't forget to treat the housing and dustbath areas as well!

Breeding problems

Reference has already been made to the necessity of having good breeding stock, and not to breed closely related strains unless you know that they are free of defects. If the introduction of females to males is carried out carefully, there is usually no problem, although it does occasionally happen that a male will refuse to accept a female. I once had a Coturnix layer which was constantly driven off by the male (she was part of a trio), and he devoted his attentions to the other one. He would not mate with her and pecked her unmercifully. I eventually had to take her and put her in solitary confinement. Her wounds healed, she seemed fit and healthy, with a good appetite, when without warning, she died. I have often wondered whether the male knew more than I did, and whether there is some selective survival mechanism which operates with discrimination in these cases.

An aspect already referred to is that breeding birds need an excellent and well-balanced diet, otherwise nutritional deficiencies may manifest in weakly chicks. Clubbed feathers and leg problems in the chicks are associated with an inadequate level of minerals and vitamins in the parent stock. (For details, see page 71).

Egg binding can sometimes be a problem. This is where a female occasionally is seen to sit for long periods of time without laying an egg. The best solution, as with other poultry, is to hold her over steam (a bowl of hot water - but take care not to drop her), and gently massage the vent with *Vaseline*. This is really all that is possible for if the egg breaks inside her, it often leads to death. Although infection is usually given as the reason why death occurs, it seems to me that shock plays a major part, for a bird can die before infection has had a chance to develop.

I have already referred to possible problems with young quail. If a good level of hygiene and incubation practice is maintained, problems will be minimised. The incubator and brooder area need complete cleaning and disinfecting after use and before a new batch of eggs and young are introduced. Most problems with poor hatches are usually connected with one of the following reasons: poor breeding stock, low fertility of parents, poor standard of nutrition in parents, or mycoplasma and other infections. Many problems in eggs are also caused by poor standards of hygiene, temperature fluctuations, humidity fluctuations or inadequate turning of the eggs.

Feather and vent pecking, and cannibalism

These are all variations of the same problem, and the causes are many and varied. Check that there is no mite problem, and that feeding and watering levels are adequate. Over-crowding and lack of interest in the environment are often contributory agents. Feeding greens helps to reduce boredom, as well as providing a wider range of nutrients. A bird which is being pecked regularly, or one that is a persistent attacker, should be separated for a time so that the habit can be broken.

Notifiable diseases

Finally, quail can be affected by Newcastle disease or Fowl pest, although it is primarily found in chickens. Symptoms are paralysis of the legs and throwing the head backwards. It is a notifiable disease in Britain so the vet or local DEFRA office should be notified. Infected flocks are normally slaughtered by the authorities, and compensation is available.

Reference Section

Books

Quail Manual. Albert F. Marsh. Marsh Farm Publications. 1976 (USA)
Quail: Their Breeding & Management. GES Robbins. WPA. 1984 (UK)
Domestic Quail for Hobby & Profit. Robbins. AB Incubators. 1989 (UK)
The Atlas of Quails. David Alderton. TFH Publications. 1992 (USA)
Raising Bobwhite Quail for Commercal Use. Circular 514. USDA 1964 (USA)
That Quail Robert. Margaret Stranger. Lippincot. 1966 (USA)
The Chinese Painted Quail. Leland B. Hayes. 1992 (USA)
The Care, Breeding & Genetics of Button Quail. Landry. Arcadia. 1998 (USA)
Upland Game Birds. Leland B. Hayes. 1997 (USA)
Quail, Past & Present. Michael Roberts. 1999 (UK)
Coturnix Quail. Edmund Hoffmann. Canada. 1988
Incubation: A Guide to Hatching & Rearing. (3rd Edition) Katie Thear.
Broad Leys Publishing Ltd. 1997 (UK)

Organisations

DEFRA Helpline: Tel: 08459 335577. www.defra.gov.uk
Humane Slaughter Association. Tel: 01582 831919. www.hsa.org.uk
World Pheasant Association. Tel: 01425 657129. www.pheasant.org.uk

Suppliers of Quail

The following were supplying quail at the time of writing. Please bear in mind that smaller breeders may only have birds available on a seasonal basis and in limited numbers so it may be necessary to order in advance.

Birdtrek. (W. Wales). Tel: 01267 281558. www.birdtrek.co.uk
Italian laying quail.

Cox (Cheshire). Tel: 07973 744848.
Italian, Japanese, Chinese Painted. Fertile eggs.

Fascinating Little Creatures (W. Yorks). www.fascinating-little-creatures.co.uk
Various mutations of Chinese Painted, Coturnix and other quail.

Fosters Poultry. (Glos). Tel: 01452 724565. www.fosterschickens.co.uk
Italian Gold, Japanese, Bobwhite. Also fertile eggs.

Game for Anything. (Devon). Tel: 01823 680092. www.gameforanything.co.uk
Jumbo, Italian and Spanish Coturnix, Colour Varieties of Coturnix, Bobwhite, Californian, Gambel's, Chinese Painted, Jungle Bush Quail. Also Fertile eggs.

Grange Aviaries & Pet Centre. (Hants). Tel: 01489 781260.
www.grangepetcentre.co.uk Chinese Painted, Bobwhite, Californian.

Greenham Quail. (Sussex). Tel: 01323 484562.
Commercial Coturnix quail and various colour strains.

Meadow View Quail. (Shropshire). Tel: 01948 880 300.
Italian laying quail, Table strains, White Range, Fawn.

Newmarket Aviaries. (Derbyshire). Tel: 01246 863506.
Italian Gold layers, Japanese, Chinese Painted (all colours), Bobwhite, Scaled quail, Californian.

Quails from Wales. (South Wales). Tel: 029 2041 1123. or 07881 557268.
www.quailsfromwales.org.uk
Japanese Coturnix in wide range of colour variations. Italian, Harlequin, Chinese Painted, Bobwhite, Mearns, Californian, Gambel's, Blue Scaled.

Equipment Suppliers

Ascott Smallholding Supplies Ltd. Tel: 0845 130 6285. www.ascott.biz
Incubators, feeders and drinkers, and equipment.

Ash and Lacy Moncasters. Tel: 01507 600666.
Wire mesh, cages and equipment.

Bamford Ltd (Lancs).Tel: 01772 456300. E-mail: sales@bamfeeds.co.uk
Quail mix feed.

Brinsea Products Ltd. Tel: 0845 226 0120. www.brinsea.co.uk
Incubators and rearing equipment.

Crediton Milling Co. Ltd. (Devon). Tel: 01363 772212. Quail feeds.

Danro Ltd. Tel: 01455 847061/2. www.danroltd.co.uk
Labels, boxes and packaging for quail eggs and other products.

The Domestic Fowl Trust. Tel: 01386 833083. www.domesticfowltrust.co.uk
Aviaries, incubators and equipment.

Ecostat Incubators. Tel: 01326 378654. www.ecostat-incubators.com
Range of incubators.

Gamekeepa Feeds Ltd. Tel: 01789 772429. www.gamekeepafeeds.co.uk
Range of incubators and equipment.

Grange Aviaries & Pet Centre (Hants).
Tel: 01489 781260. www.grangepetcentre.co.uk
Aviaries, incubators, equipment and quail feeds.

Hawthorne Animal Housing.
Tel: 0121 602 0846. www.hawthorne-animal-housing.co.uk
Housing and equipment.

Interhatch. Tel: 0700 462 8228. Range of incubators and equipment.

Manor Farm Granaries. Tel: 01832 710235. www.manor-farm-granaries.co.uk
Quail feeds, incubators and equipment.

Marriage and Sons Ltd. Tel: 01245 612000. www.marriagefeeds.co.uk
Quail feed pellets.

Optivite Ltd. (Notts). Tel: 01777 228741. www.optivite.co.uk
Vitamin/mineral pre-mixes for quail.

Solway Feeders. Tel: 01557 500253. www.solwayfeeders.com
Range of incubators, feed bins and equipment.

Patchett Engineering Ltd. (Yorks). Tel: 01274 882333. www.patchett.co.uk
Commercial quail cage systems.

Southern Aviaries. Tel: 01825 830930. www.1066.net/southernaviaries
Range of incubators and equipment.

Traditional Poultry Supplies. Tel: 01603 738292.
Range of incubators and equipment.

USA Suppliers

McMurray Hatchery Inc. (Iowa). Tel: 1-800-456-3280.
www.mcmurrayhatchery.com
Gambel's, Blue Scaled, Bobwhite. Also hatching eggs.

Lake Cumberland Game Bird Farm & Hatchery. (Kentucky). Tel: 606-348-6370.
www.lakecumberlandgamebirds.com
Jumbo, Pharoah laying quail, Gambel's, Bobwhite, Californian. Hatching
eggs.

Stromberg Hatcheries. (Minnesota). Tel: 218-587-2222.
www.strombergschickens.com
Chinese Painted, Blue Scaled, Bobwhite, Coturnix, Californian.

Pocono Quail Farm. (Pennsylvania). Tel: 570-595-9559.
www.poconoquailfarm.com
Californian, Gambel's, Blue Scaled, Mountain. Also fertile eggs.

Garrie. P. Landry. (Louisiana). Tel: 337-828-5957.
www.zebrafinch.com
Chinese Painted and colour mutations.

Index

Broad Leys Publishing Limited

specialising in poultry and smallholding books

Our other titles include the following:

Starting with Chickens. Katie Thear. £6.95

Starting with Bantams. David Scrivener. £7.95

Starting with Ducks. Katie Thear. £7.95

Starting with Geese. Katie Thear. £7.95

Incubation. Katie Thear. £6.95

Build Your Own Poultry House and Run £3.00
(A2 plans and cutting list)

Organic Poultry. Katie Thear. £12.95
(Chickens, Ducks, Geese, Turkeys, Guinea Fowl)

Starting with Turkeys. Katie Thear. (Spring 2007) £7.95

Starting with a Smallholding. David Hills. £7.95

Starting with Pigs. Andy Case. £7.95

Starting with Sheep. Mary Castell £7.95

Starting with Goats. Katie Thear. £7.95

Cheesemaking and Dairying. Katie Thear. £7.95

Starting with Bees. Peter Gordon. £7.95

Also available:

The Smallholder's Manual (Hardback). Katie Thear. £23.00

Free-Range Poultry. (Hardback). Katie Thear. £17.50

Titles may be ordered **Post-Free** (within the UK) from the publisher.

Also available from our secure on-line bookshop:
www.blpbooks.co.uk

Broad Leys Publishing Limited

1 Tenterfields, Newport, Saffron Walden, Essex CB11 3UW.
Tel/Fax: 01799 541065
E-mail: kdthear@btinternet.com